An Elementary Grammar of the Old Norse Or Icelandic Language

George Bayldon

PREFACE.

The varied and vigorous literature of ancient Scandinavia will amply repay the student for the labour which he can bestow upon it, and to facilitate his acquisition of the language in which it is embodied is the object of this little work. With this view, I have aimed at the utmost brevity consistent with completeness and precision, avoiding all those elaborate details which can only interest the advanced scholar. Stating merely those rules which must necessarily be mastered, I have endeavoured through simplicity of arrangement and a practical system to present the general structure of the Icelandic tongue before the learner's eye, so that with ordinary application it will be easily comprehended; particularly by him who possesses the advantage of an acquaintance with some of its cognate branches. Wherever rules are laid down, they are so enforced by analogous examples selected from standard authorities, with a correct translation of the passages, as to show both the proper application of them, and the right meaning of the sentences.

The earliest poetry and historical sagas of the North furnish exhaustless sources of intellectual pleasure to the antiquarian and philologist. The traditions of Iceland, carried into that island by emigrants from the Scandinavian peninsula soon after its discovery, and imperishably preserved by them in written documents, are so closely connected with the history of Northern Europe as to render a knowledge of it incomplete without them. Many of the skalds travelled in foreign lands before the twelfth century, and as they were nobles and warriors, they were received by the kings, to whom they were often related, as friends and councillors; thus on their return to their native land they brought with them much historical matter which, since the Roman characters had been introduced with the Christian religion, was committed to writing. The value of some of these documents to English history is considerable, and besides confirming or adding to our stock of facts during its darkest period, they afford us very interesting views of the state of society, and of the manners and mode of living of the age in which they were composed.

After the departure of the Roman legions from this country, the Jutes, Saxons, and Angles, who occupied respectively Jutland in Denmark, the district between the Elbe and the Eyder, and Anglen in the south-east part of the Duchy of Slesvik, successively obtained settlements in Britain. The language which resulted from this blended colonization, marked however by strong dialectic variations, is generally styled Anglo-Saxon, which term was first introduced by Asser, in his Life of Alfred. The resemblance between it and the Old Norse, as is to be expected, is striking, since both are the offspring of that primitive tongue, the Gothic, spoken by the ancestors of all the Teutonic tribes. For instance, the Anglo-Saxon letter *th* is common to both Icelandic and English, though unknown to most of the allied dialects. The article, noun, adjective and pronoun are alike declinable in Anglo-Saxon and Old Norse, having different forms for the three genders, for the four cases, and for the singular and plural numbers; besides which, the pronoun of the first and second persons has a dual, or form exclusively appropriated to the number two. The adjective has two forms of inflection; the one employed when the adjective is used without a determinative, the other when it is preceded by an article or a pronoun agreeing also with the noun. These forms are called, respectively, the indefinite and definite. The verbs have four moods; the indicative, subjunctive, imperative and infinitive, and but two tenses, the present and the past. In both languages the definite article partakes very strongly of its original character of a demonstrative pronoun. The nouns have three genders, and the masculine and feminine are often applied to objects incapable of sex.

Furthermore, Icelandic, from its close relationship to Anglo-Saxon, furnishes more abundant analogies for the illustration of obscure English etymological and syntactical forms than any other of the kindred tongues. "It is but recently", says Marsh in his Lectures on the English Language, "that the great value of Icelandic philology has become known to the other branches of the Gothic stock, and one familiar with the treasures of that remarkable literature, and the wealth, power, and flexibility of the language which contains it, sees occasion to regret the want of a thorough knowledge of it in English and American grammatical writers, more frequently than of any other attainment whatever".

The incursions which the piratical Danes and Norwegians, by whom Iceland was colonized, made upon the shores of Britain, supply our history with many important incidents during the two centuries immediately preceding the Norman Conquest. Along with their peculiar customs and superstitions, these sea-kings introduced several words and phrases into our language, which have left their impress up to the present time chiefly on the northern dialects of the English peasantry. Many provincialisms are thus retained by them the etymology of which can be traced to a Scandinavian origin. The following, selected from a large number, will sufficiently illustrate this statement.

Provincialisms.	English.	Icelandic.
bain	near	beinn
bawk	a cross beam	bálkr
beck	brook.	bekkr
bigg	barley	bygg
duck	cloth	dúkr
eldin	kindling	elding
fell	mountain	fjall
to flit	to remove	flytja
force	waterfall	fors
frosk	frog	froskr
garth	enclosure (yard)	garðr
*gaum*less	half silly	gaumr (*heed*)
gill	cleft	gil
to girn	to yearn	girna
gowk	cuckoo	gaukr
to grave	to dig	grafa
to harry	to plunder	herja
hegg	bird-cherry	heggr
host	cough	hosti
ing	meadow	eng
kitling	kitten	kettlingr
to lake	to play	leika
lathe	barn	hlaða
lift	air	lopt
ling	heather	lyng
muck	dung	myki
neive	fist	hnefi
puck	goblin	púki
rang	wrong	rangr
rig	back	hryggr
to rive	to tear in pieces	rífa

Provincialisms.	English.	Icelandic.
royd	cleared space	rjóðr
sackless	simple	saklauss
scatte	tax	skattr
skuggy	gloomy	skuggi (*shade*)
to speer	to ask	spyrja
to steven	to bespeak	stefna
tale	number	tala
to thole	to endure	þola
to wale	to choose	velja
wark	pain	verkr.

In the midland northern districts of England where the Danes and Norwegians mostly settled, a considerable number of places with names of Scandinavian descent, are to be found, such as:

			Old Norse.	
Whit*by*,	meaning,	*white village*	býr,	first, *a farm*, then, *a town*.
Bracken-*thwaite*,	—	*fern land*	þveit,	*detached piece of land*.
Nor*thorpe*,	—	*north village*	þorp,	*cluster of houses*.
Angles*ey*,	—	*Angles' island*	ey,	*island*.
Caith*ness*,	—	*naze of Catuibh* (its ancient Gaelic name)	næs,	*promontory*.
Stor*with*,	—	*large wood*	viðr,	*wood*.
Lang*toft*,	—	*long field*	toft,	*field near a farm*.
Field*garth*,	—	*mountain farm*	garðr,	*enclosure, yard*.
Green*wich*,	—	*pine bay*	vikr,	*bay*.
South*wark*,	—	*southern fort*	virki,	*fortress*.

A thorough study of Scandinavian literature would elucidate many points in our early history which are now obscure, particularly that portion of it comprised in the Anglo-Saxon period; and since the Icelandic language is so closely akin to Anglo-Saxon, the parent of our own, it seems evident that some proficiency in it should be sought by every educated Englishman who wishes to possess a complete knowledge of his mother-tongue. Should the present work in any way prove an auxiliary in so useful a pursuit, or induce the student to enter a comparatively unexplored region of interesting lore, the author will have gained his principal aim.

INDEX.

PART I.

PART II.

PART III.

PART IV.

ERRATA.

Page		Line	
5	. .	11,	*for* Is *read* Ice.
9	. .	29,	— there *r.* these.
19	. .	12,	— Svörð *swoord r.* Svörðr *sward.*
27	. .	22,	— flar *r.* flœr.
28	. .	10,	— hjörtna *r.* hjartna.
35	. .	17,	— eignar-nar *r.* eignir-nar.
38	. .	19,	— form *r.* forms.
44	. .	7,	— litinn *r.* lítinn.
49	. .	37,	— okkaru *r.* okkarn.
50	. .	9,	— váru *r.* várn.
53	. .	22,	— nökkur-u *r.* nökkur-n.
55	. .	12,	— 11 *r.* 13.
55	. .	24,	— *fortymen r. forty men.*
56	. .	16,	— tuttugast *r.* tuttugasti.
61	. .	30,	— *embúinn r. em búinn.*
63	. .	5,	— bra *r.* brá.
64	. .	11,	— lang *r.* long.
68	. .	15,	— frysum *r.* frysim.
68	. .	16,	— frysuð *r.* frysið.
68	. .	17,	— frysu *r.* frysi.
70	. .	35,	— höggvin *r.* höggvinn.
77	. .	16,	— þraðr *r.* þráðr.
89	. .	32,	— rikr *r.* ríkr.
98	. .	24,	— allter *r.* allt er.
101	. .	8,	— 89 *r.* 84.
101	. .	12,	— iss *r.* íss.
113	. .	31,	— in *r.* no.

PART I.

ORTHOGRAPHY.

CHAPTER I.

LETTERS AND PRONUNCIATION.

The Icelandic Alphabet consists of the following letters: a, b, c, d, ð, e, f, g, h, i, j, k, l, m, n, o, œ, p, q, r, s, t, u, v, x, y, z, þ, ö, æ.

The vowels are:

a, ö, æ, e, i, o, œ, u, y.

Of these, a, e, i, o, u, y can be lengthened by accents, and thus the following are short:

a, e, i, o, u, y, ö;

and the following long:

á, è, í, ó, ú, ý, æ.

a is pronounced like *a* in *fat, father*.
á » » » *oa* in *broad;* or *a* in *warm*.
ö » » » *i* or *u* in *girdle, first, murder, sun*.
æ » » » the English long *i*.
e » » » *e* in *met*.
è » » » *e* in *there*.
i » » » *i* in *bill*.
í » » » *ee* in *bee*.
o » » » *o* in *not*.
ó » » » *o* in *fore*, or rather broader.
œ » » » *a* in *paper*.
u » » » *iew* in *view*.

ú is pronounced like *oo* in *rood.*
y » » » *i* in *pill.*
ý » » » *ee* in *peel.*

---

a, á, o, ó, u, ú, are called hard vowels, and ö, æ, e, è, i, í, œ, y, ý, soft.

Sound and Power of Vowels.

A — This letter, as noticed above, is pronounced like *a* in *fat,* when short. *Example,* askr *ash-tree:* when long and unaccented, like *a* in *father. Ex.,* saga *a tale.* On the Faroe it has frequently a sound approaching to *ā* (English *a*).

Á — Like *oa* in *broad,* or *a* in *warm. Ex.,* háls *neck.* It answers to the Danish *aa* and the Swedish å. In words where *á* follows *v* (for instance, vápn *weapon,* vár *spring,* ván *hope*) the Icelanders often use *o.*

Ö — Like *i* or *u* in *girdle, first, murder, sun. Ex.,* örn *eagle.* This letter is mostly only a vowel change of *a* which belongs to that class of vowels capable of being softened or modified by a change of their original sounds. It is the Danish short *ø,* and Swedish *ö,* and sounds much as the French *eu* in *peu.* It was introduced at a comparatively late period into the Old Norse alphabet, the diphthong *au* being written for it in ancient manuscripts.

Æ — Like the English long *i. Ex.,* æfi *lifetime.* Its sound might be represented by the letters *aj,* which the Icelanders would pronounce like the German *ei.* In Norway, on the other hand, as in modern Danish, it sounds like our *a* in *paper.* In the ancient writings both modes alternate; the former, however, has most in its favour, and it is perhaps the oldest. In most cases *æ* is only a modified vowel.

E — Like *e* in *met. Ex.,* elska *to love.*

È — Like *e* in *there. Ex.,* mèr *to me.* This letter is often written with a grave accent. Besides determining the pronunciation of the vowel, this accent serves to prevent confusion in the meaning of many words. For instance:

vel *well*, and vèl *guile*.
her *army*, and hèr *here*.
el *feeds*, and èl *hailstorm*.
fell *fell* (s.), and fèll *fell* (v.).
fletta *to cleave*, and flètta *to plait*.
let *dissuades*, and lèt *let*.
setti *placed*, and sètti *seventh* (modern; sjötti).
lek *leaks* (v.), and lèk *played*.

The ancient Faroese manuscripts, instead of *è*, sometimes used *ea*; *e. g.* nea = è.

I — Like *i* in *bill*. *Ex.*, viss *certain*. With this letter *e* is often interchanged in old writings, especially in the endings of words, as, lande for landi *landsman*, misser for missir *loss*. The vowel *y* is frequently used instead of *i*, *e. g.*, mykill for mikill *much* or *great*; but this variation occurs chiefly in the definite form (hinn mykli *the great*).

Í — Like *ee* in *bee*. *Ex.*, vísa *song*. In the noun-termination *i* which has the genitive in *ja*, and therefore stands instead of *ji*, this vowel is pronounced by the modern Icelanders like *yee*; *e. g.* vilí, pronounced vilji (vilyee). Sometimes the termination of a proper noun in *-in*, when it takes the place of *-yn*, is pronounced like *yin*, *e. g.*, Skõðin like Skõðyin, Tõðin like Tõðyin.

O — Like *o* in *not*, when short. *Ex.*, hopp *hop, leap*. When long and unaccented, somewhat like *oo* in *pool*. *Ex.*, hola *cave*.

Ó — This vowel takes a deep sound, rather broader than *o* in *fore*. *Ex.*, ró *rest*.

[Œ — Like *a* in *paper*. *Ex.*, œxl *increase*. It frequently becomes a vowel-change of *ó*.]

U — Like *iew* in *view*. *Ex.*, kul *airing*. Its pronunciation resembles that of the French *u* in *du*, and the German *ü* in *Hüte*. Ö is often used for *u*, but mostly in the endings of words, *e. g.*, hèröð for hèruð *district*.

Ú — Like *oo* in *rood*. *Ex.*, hús *house*. Formerly *u* and *v* were interchangeable letters as in English; but they are now used separately.

Y — Like *i* in *pill*. *Ex.*, lyng *ling, heath*. In consequence of its sound it alternates with *i* in many instances. It is related in pronunciation to ý, as *i* is to *í*. The most valuable ancient Mss. constantly make a distinction between *y* and ý. *Y* is in most cases only a modified *u*, or more rarely *o*. In certain words, principally particles, *y* and *i* are interchanged; for instance, fyrir and firir *for*, yfir and ifir *over*.

Ý — Like *ee* in *peel*. *Ex.*, mýri *moor*.

The lengthened vowels á, è, í, ó, ú, ý, and the vowel-changes æ and œ may be regarded as a species of diphthong, at least as respects the pronunciation. Agreeably to orthography, *au*, *ey* and *ei* are proper diphthongs.

au is pronounced like *oy* in *boy*. *Ex.*, auga *eye*.

ey, a modified *au* approaches the German *eu*, having a broader sound than our word *eye*. It is pronounced much in the same way as the pronoun *I* in several of our provincial dialects — in the North Staffordshire, for instance. It is often interchanged with *ei*. The older sound, which still obtains in Norway, is *øi*.

ei is pronounced very close, rather like *ei* in *weight*; but never as the German *ei* in *Stein*, *Bein*. In Old Swedish *ei* is sounded like *è*.

CHAPTER II.

CONSONANTS.

The consonants are:

b, c, d, ð, f, g, h, j, k, l, m, n, p, q, r, s, t, þ, v, x, z.

They are divided, according to the organs by which they are pronounced, — the throat, tongue, and lips, into gutturals, linguals, and labials.

Some are distinguished by the name of liquids, because they readily unite with the mute consonants, and flow into their sounds.

The following is their classification:

Gutturals: g, k, j.
Linguals: d, t, þ, ð, s.
Labials: b, p, f, v.
Liquids: l, m, n, r.

The letters *c*, *q*, *x*, *z* must be classed as hard mutes.

The spirant *h*, being formed by the breath merely, does not belong to any of the articulating organs in particular.

The consonants *c, s, z* are also called sibilants, from the hissing nature of their sounds.

B is pronounced as in English.

C is often found in the oldest manuscripts, as in Anglo-Saxon, instead of *k*, and is therefore sounded like that letter. There is no instance in which *k* may not be used in its place.

D is pronounced as in English.

Ð, ð (called in Islandic *eð*) has a strongly rolling sound, and never occurs at the beginning of words. It is an aspirated or weak *d* or dh, and always sounds soft, as *th* in *this*, *bathe*. *Ex.*, gjörði *did*. It is never doubled, but is changed into *dd*, as: gleð, gladdi, ryð, ruddi.

F is sounded at the beginning of a syllable and before *s* as in English; *e. g.*, fótr *foot*, ofsi *arrogance*: at the end of a word it is pronounced like hard *v*, *e. g.*, haf *sea*, when it is often written *v*, which is likewise the case in the Faroese language: *stevni*, *stevndi*, *stevnt*. It has also the hard sound before *r* (ur), as hafr *he-goat*, and between all vowels in the middle of a word, *e. g.* hafa *to have*. Before *l, n*, *ð*, *t*, at the end of a syllable, this sound of *v* passes over to *b* or *bb*; *e. g.*, afl (pron. abl.) *strength*, nafn (nabbn) *name*. If another consonant, especially *d* or *t*, follow after *fn*, the sound becomes *mn*; *e. g.*, nefna *to name*, is pronounced nābbna, but nefndi *named*, like nāmndi, and nefnt *named* (past part.), as nāmnt. This pronunciation is general when *d* follows; but if the succeeding consonant be *t* or *s*, it is often sounded as fft, ffs, *e. g.*, jafnt, til jafns (jafft, jaffs). Where *f* is to be pronounced hard in the middle of a word, it is doubled, *e. g.*, offra *to offer*, in distinction from ofra *to swing*, which is read *ovra*.

G is sounded as in English before *a, o, u* and *au*. *G* and *gj* before *e, i, y, æ, œ, ö, ey, ei*, are sounded soft like the Danish *gj*, or English *gu* in *guard*, with a slight after-sound of *j*; as, gefa *to give*, gæfi *might give*, geir *spear*. If a vowel go before, and a soft one or *j* come after, it sounds like *y* consonant, *e. g.*, bogi *a bow*, agi *chastisement*, fægja *to smooth*, bágindi *troubles* (pronounced boyi, ayi, faiya, boayindi). At the end of syllables after a long vowel it was aspirated in former times, and therefore written *gh*, as: lŏgh *law*, vegh *weigh*. Its sound must thus have been very feeble, as in this case it is almost entirely omitted in the present Norwegian pronunciation, *e. g.*, *drag*, pronounced dra, *dag*, da. If another consonant follow *gn*, especially *d* or *t*, the sound becomes *ngn*; for instance, lygna *to grow calm*, is heard nearly like liggna, but the imperfect lygndi is pronounced lingndi or lingdi, and lygnt like lingnt or lingt; but should *s* follow, the sound resembles *ggs*; *e. g.*, til gagns (gaggs) *for gain*.

H is always aspirated, and has a hard and strong sound before *j*, *v*, *l*, *n*, *r*; *e. g.*, hjarta *heart*, hverfa *to turn*, hlaða *to load*, hnŏttr *bowl*, hringr *ring*. It is occasionally interchanged with *k* before *n*; *e. g.*, knífr and hnífr *knife*, and some more words.

J is sounded like the German *j* or our *y* consonant. It is only a short or consonantal *i*, and should therefore be entirely rejected in most cases, and supplanted by it. In old manuscripts, moreover, we find *e* where *j* is now used; *e. g.*, earl = jarl *earl*, seálfr = sjálf *self*.

K is pronounced at the end of a syllable, before a consonant and the vowels *a*, *o* and *u*, as in English. It is also generally written for *ch*, *e. g.*, kristr, kór, and is often used instead of *g*; *e. g.*, kvikr *living*. It is likewise doubled in place of *ck*; *e. g.*, plokka or plocka *to pluck*. *K* and *kj* before *e*, *i*, *y*, *æ*, *œ*, *ŏ*, *ey*, *ei* are sounded soft like the Danish *kj* with a slight after-sound of *j*, resembling *c* in the English words *care*, *cure*. It is never pronounced like *ch* in *church*, which is the case with the Swedish soft *k*. In the plural of substantives in *andi* derived from verbs in *ga* or *ka* (without *j*), *g* or *k* preceding *e* has its hard sound; *e. g.*, from eiga *to own* comes eigandi *owner*, plural eigendr (pronounced eigăndr), elskandi *lover*, plur. elskendr (pronounced elskăndr). *Sk* has the sound of *sc* in our word *scare* before *a*, *o*, *u*, and of *sh* before *e*, *i* in root-syllables.

L, as a single letter, is sounded as in English. When double, it is pronounced by the Icelanders and West Norwegians, as well as by the Faroese, like *dl*; *e. g.*, kalla (pronounced kadla) *to call*; consequently it is sometimes interchanged with *dl*; *e. g.*, á milli or á midli *between*, from mið *in the midst*. But in cases where *d*, *t*, or *s* follows, *e. g.*, felldi *felled*, allt *all*, alls *of all*, and also in compound words and derivatives where each *l* belongs to a separate syllable, *e. g.*, til-lag *contribution*, Hal-land *Holland*, mikil-látr *high-minded*, *ll* is sounded as in English. *Rl* has a rolling sound much like that of the hard *ll* heard almost as *rdl*, *e. g.*, jarl *earl*. In certain districts of South Norway, especially West Tellemarken and Sætersdal, *ll* is pronounced like *dd*; *e. g.*, gull (properly gudl) *gold*, in Sætersdal gudd. In many parts of Norway *l* is not heard before a mute consonant with a long vowel before it: *e. g.*, kálf (pronounced kaav) *calf*, úlf (úv) *wolf*, fólk (fók) *folk*. This pronunciation prevails in Tellemarken and Sætersdal.

M sounds as in English.

N, single, sounds as in English: double, it is pronounced after *á*, *é*, *í*, *ei*, *ó*, *ú*, *æ* and *œ* as *dn*; *e. g.*, steinn (steidn) *stone*. But if *nn* belong to the following syllable, or if a simple vowel precede it, the sound is the same as in English; *e. g.*, á-nni *to the river*, ey-nni *to the island*, kanna *to examine*, brenna *to burn*. *Rn* has a rolling sound, somewhat like *rdn*, making the antecedent vowel very hard and sharp; *e. g.*, horn (hordn) *horn*.

P as in English. Before *t* like *f*; *e. g.*, eptir (pronounced eftir) *after*: consequently *ft* has been latterly much used in place of *pt*. In many districts of Norway and in the Faroe, *p* is entirely assimilated with the succeeding *t*, where *eptir* is pronounced *ettir*. No word beginning with *p* is of genuine Norse origin.

Q is to be met with in its ordinary place before *v*, and used to alternate with *k*, but in the Old Norse alphabet it is a superfluous letter.

R is mostly sounded as in English. For its pronunciation before *l* and *n* see remarks under those letters. *R* answers to three forms in the ancient language; namely, to *r* pure, to *s*, which is also found written in the oldest manuscripts, and occurs in the Gothic: *e. g.*, vesa *or* vera *to be* (Anglo-Saxon wesan), heysa *or* heyra *to hear*, meisi *or* meiri *more*, and lastly, in the beginning of words, to *vr*, *e. g.*, ríta *to write*, originally vríta, reiði *wrath*, formerly vreiði, rangr *wrong*, anciently vrangr. These forms occur in Old Swedish, but have disappeared in Norsk, where, on the other hand, we sometimes find in *r* a fixed sound of *v* signified by *u* added, rueiði for reiði, ruangr for rangr. This form of *v* has again appeared in the written tongue, and partly in the modern pronunciation. When the *r* alone forms a kind of syllable by itself, *e. g.*, in most nominative endings in the masculine, in genitives singular and nominatives and accusatives plural in the feminine, and in the second and third persons singular in the present indicative of the irregular conjugations, it is pronounced by the Icelanders and Faroese as *ur*, *e. g.*, maður for maðr, stendur for stendr, merkur for merkr. In former times it seems to have been sounded arbitrarily; in Norway, mostly *er*: hence we often find written maðer, goðer; and also as *ar* (maðar, konungar).

S has always the hard sound of *ss* in *miss*. It interchanges with *ls* in some words, as: gisl gils, beisl beils.

T as in English. *Tns* is pronounced at the end of words like *s*.

Þ (called in Icelandic *Thorn*) is an aspirated *t* (*th*), as ð is an aspirated *d* (*dh*). It is pronounced like the Greek *θ*, and the English *th* in *think*, *e. g.*, þeinkja *to think*, except in pronouns, or particles which are attracted like enclitics to the foregoing word; *e. g.*, á æfi þinni *in thy days*, erþ'at (for þú at), where it has the sound of ð, dependent, however, on the preceding letter. This consonant is only found at the beginning of a word, and is consequently never doubled.

V sounds as in English. It is partly a consonantal *u*, and bears the same relation to this vowel as *j* to *i*; partly an independent consonant, which is to be regarded as a softening of *f* occurring in cognate words, either in the language itself, or in the other dialects. This difference, which is etymologically important, does not concern the pronunciation.

X as in English.

Z is to be mostly regarded as an etymological sign which sometimes represents *st*, *ds* or *ts*; thus we find both *beraz* and *berast*, *æðstr* and *æztr*, *bestr* and *beztr*, *kvaðst*, *kvazt* and *kvaz*. Properly, it is only used instead of *ðs* and *ts*, and is then always sounded like *s*.

CHAPTER III.

ACCENTUATION.

In a word of more than one syllable, a greater stress is naturally placed on one syllable than on another, and in a combination of words, one word is pronounced with greater force than another. For instance, in the words *hestar, ljúga, öndvegi,* the syllables *hest, ljúg* and *önd* are uttered with greater force than those which follow them. In the sentences hann stökk yfir garðinn *he sprang over the fence;* eg talaði leingi við hann *I talked a long time with him,* a greater stress is laid on the words *garðinn, leingi,* than on those with which they are connected. This is called the grammatical accent; but *emphasis* is essentially different from accent. In the latter case the speaker lays stress on some particular word or syllable which in itself may be of less importance, but which, for certain reasons, he wishes to render emphatic. Take the examples cited above: *hann* stökk &c., *he* sprang, &c.; *eg* talaði, &c., *I* spoke, &c.

The first syllable always takes the chief tone, whether the words be long or short, compound or simple. In dissyllabic words the final syllable is consequently short, *e. g.,* brēnnă *to burn.* In trisyllabics the penultimate has a stronger tone than the last; *e. g.,* kāllāðĭ *called,* fēlăgĭ *fellow.* But when the last member of a compound or derivative is monosyllabic, the final syllable has a stronger tone than the middle; *e. g.,* hōfŭð hōf *chief temple,* ūpprūnălĭgt *original.* Polysyllabic words have the lesser tone on the penultimate, *e. g.,* köngurváfa *spider.*

Some prepositions, *e. g.,* ámóti *against,* ámilli *between,* ígegnum *through,* seem to form an exception to the rule that the chief tone always rests on the first syllable; but there are properly only compounds of two words which are better written separately, á móti, á milli, í gegnum; consequently, the first part, or real preposition, is omitted in all compounds formed with these words, *e. g.,* mótganga *enmity,* meðalaùki *compensation.*

R or *ur* final is regarded as a short syllable which is very rarely reckoned in metrical composition. It has a faint sound of *ur* or *er; e. g.,* maðr *man,* góðr *good.*

Words of foreign origin, of which few however have been adopted into the Old Norse, as a rule are pronounced and accented according to the sound and tone peculiar to them in their native tongues; *e. g.*, pistill from *epistola*, postuli *apostulus*.

Foreign words are often contracted, *e. g.*, tempra *tempero*; lína *linea*; regla *regula*.

The first unaccented syllable is often rejected; spitali, postuli, biskup *episcopus*.

A vowel before a simple consonant becomes somewhat lengthened, whether the consonant be hard or soft, as: ēk or ēg, sēt, lās. When the short sound is expressed, the consonant is doubled, as: egg, sett, hlass.

Vowels are sounded short when a consonant is added, as:

lǫ̈g	has a long ǫ̈	—	lǫ̈gǒum	a short one.
kef	» » » e	—	kefja	» » »
vil	» » » i	—	vildi	» » »

All consonants which follow a vowel belong to the syllable containing it, as: ask-a, mold-igr, skip-in-u. Hence the words are rendered short at the end of a line in poetry.

J and *v*, which belong to the vowel following them, form exceptions, as: spyr-jum, dǫ́gg-va. The letter *r* is mostly read with the next vowel, as: ham-rar *hammers*.

Proper names, as Sigurðr, Noregr, were always written with capital letters; but guð *God*, djǫ̈full *devil*, konungr *king*, jarl *earl*, and such like, with small initials.

CHAPTER IV.

VOWEL-CHANGE.

Besides the proper endings, a change of vowel within the word itself frequently takes place, corresponding with the German *umlaut*, and this modification of vowels constitutes an important element in the declension and derivation of words. Compare:

	Anglo-Saxon.	English.	German.	Icelandic.
sing.	fót	foot	fuss	fótr
plur.	fét	feet	füsse	fœtr.

The vowels are divided into two classes, namely, the A-class which contains *a, ǫ̈, e, i, á, æ, ei* (and *ja, já, jæ, jǫ̈, è, ì*), and the O-class which comprises *o, u, y, ó, ú, ý, au, ey* (and *jó, jú*).

A is changed:

1. into *ö* in the chief syllable before endings in *u*, as: saga, sögu;
   in the chief syllable of polysyllables, the others taking *u*, as: bakari, bökurum;
   in neutr. plur. of nouns with consonantal endings, as: haf, höf; land, lönd;
   in neutr. plur. of adjectives with consonantal endings, as: glað, glöð;
   in fem. sing. of adjectives with consonantal endings, as: hagr, hög.
2. into *e* in derivatives, as: lenda from land, nefna from nafn;
   before the endings *i* and *r*, as: dagr, degi, faðir, feðr;
   in the monosyllabic pres. 1st pers. sing. of verbs in the 3rd conj., as: taka, tek.
3. into *á* in the imp. 1st pers. plur. of verbs in the 2nd conj., as: drap, drápum.
4. into *u* in the imp. 1st pers. plur. of verbs in the 1st conj., as: braun, brunnum.

E is changed:

1. into *a* in the monosyllabic imp. 1st pers. sing. of verbs in the 1st and 2nd conj., as: bell, ball.
2. into *i*, as: regna, rignir.
3. into *i*, in derivatives, as: virða from verð.
4. into *á* in the monosyl. imp. 1st pers. sing. of verbs in 1st and 2nd conj., as: bregð, brá; fregn, frá.
5. into *ó* in the monosyl. imp. 1st pers. sing. of verbs in 3rd conj., as: dreg, dró.

I is changed:

into *a* in the monosyl. imp. 1st pers. sing. of verbs in the 1st conj., as: finn, fann.

Á is changed:

1. into *e* in the past part. of verbs in the 2nd conj., as: drápum, drepinn;
2. into *o* in the past part. of verbs in the 1st conj., as: stálum, stolinn;
3. into *æ* before the endings *i* and *r*, as: þráðr, þræði, þræðir.

Ŏ is changed:

1. into *a* before endings which contain *a*, as: sakar, saka from sŏk;
2. into *e* before the endings *i* and *r*: as: berki, merkr;
3. into *y*, in derivatives, as: smyrja from smjŏr.

Ei is changed:

1. into *i* in the monosyl. imp. 1st pers. plur. of verbs in the 4th conj., as: beið, biðum;
2. into *i* in derivatives, as: hiti from heitr.

Ja is changed into *i*, as: bjarnar, birni; and into *jŏ*, as: djarf, djŏrf.

Jŏ is changed into *i*, as: djŏrf, dirfast.

Of the O-class of vowels are changed, O:

1. into *y*, as: son, synir; of, yfir;
2. into *e*, as: hnot, hnetr. This change is of rare occurrence.

U is changed:

1. into *o* in the past part. of verbs in the 1st and 5th conj., burgum, borginn, hrutum, hrotinn;
2. into *y*, as: guð, gyðja.

Ó is changed:

1. into *æ* (*œ*), as: kló, klær;
2. into *y* in derivatives, as: fylki from fólk.

Ú is changed:

into ý, as: mús, mýs, and in derivatives. as: hýða from húð.

Au is changed:

1. into *ey*, as: laus, leysa;
2. into *u*, as: lauk, lukum;
3. into *o*, in derivatives, as: dropi from draup.

Jó is changed into ý, as: brjóta, brýt.

Jú is changed into ý, as: ljúga, lýgi.

Ndt is assimilated in short words to *tt*, as: batt, *bandt*.

Ngk is assimilated in short words to *kk*, as: sprakk, *sprang*.

Nr is assimilated in short words to *nn*, as: sýnn, *sýnr*.

Lr is assimilated in short words to *ll*, as: heill, *heilr*.

V is rejected before *o*, *u*, *y*, and *r* at the beginning of words, as, from *verpa* is formed *varp*, which in the different parts of the verb is changed into *orpinn*, *urpum* and *yrpi*. Before the word *reiði*, which used to be written *vreiði*, the consonant *v* is likewise dropt.

PART II.

ETYMOLOGY.

CHAPTER I.

INFLECTED WORDS.

The parts of speech which are subject to inflection or terminational change are, articles, nouns, adjectives, pronouns, by declension, and verbs by conjugation.

THE ARTICLE.

The indefinite article *a* or *an*, or the numeral *one*, has three genders, and four cases, and is thus declined:

	SINGULAR.			PLURAL.		
	Masc.	Fem.	Neut.	Masc.	Fem.	Neut.
Nom.	einn	ein	eitt	einir	einar	ein
Gen.	eins	einnar	eins	einna	einna	einna
Dat.	einum	einni	einu	einum	einum	einum
Acc.	einn	eina	eitt	eina	einar	ein

Used in the plural number, this word has mostly the sense of *some*.

The definite article *the* is thus declined:

	SING.			PLUR.		
	Masc.	Fem.	Neut.	Masc.	Fem.	Neut.
Nom.	hinn	hin	hitt	hinir	hinar	hin
Gen.	hins	hinnar	hins	hinna	hinna	hinna
Dat.	hinum	hinni	hinu	hinum	hinum	hinum
Acc.	hinn	hina	hitt	hina	hinar	hin.

This word is also used as a demonstrative pronoun in the signification of *that*. When appended to a substantive it constitutes its definite inflected form, as: maðr-inn *the man*, eik-in *the oak*, dyr-it *the animal;* but *h* is then always left out, and one *t* in the neuter.

The vowel *i* itself is dropt when the word ends in a simple vowel, as: indefinite *tunga*, definite *tungan* (not *tunga-in* or *tungin*) ; but if the noun terminate in a consonant, then *i* is retained, except in the nominative plural masculine, and nominative and accusative plural feminine.

Appended to nouns it takes the following endings:

	SING.			PLUR.		
	Masc.	Fem.	Neut.	Masc.	Fem.	Neut.
Nom.	-inn	-in	-it *or* ið	-nir	-nar	-in
Gen.	-ins	-innar (-nnar)	-ins	-nna	-nna	-nna
Dat.	-num	-inni (-nni)	-nu	-num	-num	-num
Acc.	-inn	-ina (-na)	-it *or* ið	-na	-nar	-in.

In the dative plural the *m* at the end of the noun is omitted when the article is added, for the sake of euphony as, *flotunum* for flötum-num. The definite article is placed before adjectives in the definite inflected form, as: hinn góði *the good.*

CHAPTER II.

THE NOUN.

Nouns, or Substantives, have three genders, Masculine, Feminine, and Neuter, and two numbers, Singular and Plural, with four cases in each, Nominative, Genitive, Dative, and Accusative.

It is impossible to give infallible rules for gender, but the following remarks may be of use.

Masculines commonly end in *i, r, l, n,* or *s,* though all nouns with these terminations are not necessarily of that gender.

The names of the duties and employments of men are masculine, *e. g.,* konungr *king,* höfðingi *chieftain,* prestr *priest,* þræll *thrall.*

Words ending in *dómr, ungr, ingr, ingi, leikr, skapr, naðr, ari* and *andi* are masculine.

Compound words retain the gender of their last part, which is also the case with the names of countries and towns; *e. g.,* Noregr (Norvegr) *Norway,* and Mikligarðr *Constantinople* are masculine, their last members *vegr* and *garðr* being so; Danmörk *Denmark,* Svíþjód *Sweden,* and Slèsvik are feminine, as *mörk, þjód,* and *vik* are of this gender; and þýzkaland *Germany,* as well as Sviaríki *Sweden,* are neuter since they terminate in neuter nouns.

The gender of Icelandic substantives may likewise be ascertained to some extent by that of nouns in the cognate languages.

The names of the duties and employments of women are feminine as, drottning *queen*, ljósa *midwife*, ambátt *she-slave*.

All substantives in *a* are feminine, *e.g.*, gata *path*, haka *chin*; except herra *master* (German *Herr*), and síra *sire*, and some proper names, which are masculine, as Sturla, as well as the neuter nouns comprised in the seventh declension.

Most monosyllabic substantives whose root-vowel is *ö* are feminine; *e.g.*, gröf *a ditch*, vök *an ice-hole*, skör *a stair-step*; though some neuters must be excepted; *e.g.*, fjör *life-strength*, böl *bale*, tröll *ogre*, kjör *choice*, kvöld *evening*.

Words ending in *ung*, *ing*, *un*, *a*, *ð*, *ska*, *sla*, *átta*, and most in *an*, *ni*, are feminine.

All monosyllabic nouns having the vowel *a*, but not ending in *r*, *l*, *n*, or *s*, are neuter, *e. g.*, malt *malt*, land *country*, haf *sea*, lag *a layer*.

DECLENSION OF NOUNS.

The number of declensions is eight.

FIRST DECLENSION.

This contains all masculine nouns in *-l*, *-n*, *-r*, *-s*, in the nominative, and *-s* in the genitive singular.

SING.	*nom.*	-r, -l, -n, -s	PLUR.	*nom.*	-ar, -ir
	gen.	-s		*gen.*	-a
	dat.	-i, or the root.		*dat.*	-um
	acc.	the root.		*acc.*	-a, -i.

Paradigms: hestr, hamarr, þyrnir, hvalr, engill, sveinn, báss.

SING.	*nom.*	hestr *a horse*	PLUR.	*nom.*	hestar *horses*
	gen.	hests *of a horse*		*gen.*	hesta *of horses*
	dat.	hesti *to a horse*		*dat.*	hestum *to horses*
	acc.	hest *a horse.*		*acc.*	hesta *horses.*

SINGULAR.

	A hammer.	*A thorn.*	*A whale.*	*An angel.*	*A swain.*	*A stall.*
N.	hamarr	þyrnir	hvalr	engill	sveinn	báss
G.	hamars	þyrnis	hvals	engils	sveins	báss
D.	hamri	þyrni	hval	engli	sveini	bási
A.	hamar	þyrni	hval	engil	svein	bás

PLURAL.

	hammers.	*thorns.*	*whales.*	*angels.*	*swains.*	*stalls.*
N.	hamrar	þyrnar	hvalir	englar	sveinar	básar
G.	hamra	þyrna	hvala	engla	sveina	bása
D.	hömrum	þyrnum	hvölum	englum	sveinum	básum
A.	hamra	þyrna	hvali	engla	sveina	bása.

Like *hestr* are declined

Álfr *elf.*
Almr *elm.*
Arfr *inheritance.*
Armr *arm.*
Askr *ash.*
Aurr *sandy bottom.*
Bátr *boat.*
Baugr *ring.*
Bjórr *beaver.*
Brandr *sword.*
Broddr *goad.*
Brunnr *well.*
Bukkr *buck.*
Dómr *doom.*
Draugr *spectre.*
Draumr *dream.*
Dúkr *cloth.*
Dvergr *dwarf.*
Eiðr *oath.*
Eldr *fire.*
Faðmr *fathom.*
Faldr *head-dress.*
Fiskr *fish.*
Flokkr *flock.*
Fnjóskr *thrush.*
Forkr *fork.*
Froskr *frog.*
Gaddr *spike.*
Gammr *vulture.*
Garðr *farm-house.*
Gaukr *cuckoo.*
Gaumr *heed.*
Geirr *spear.*
Gluggr *window.*
Hallr *stone.*
Hálmr *straw.*
Hampr *hemp.*
Haugr *heap.*
Haukr *hawk.*
Heggr *bird-cherry.*
Heimr *home.*
Herr *host.*
Hleifr *loaf.*
Hnúkr *mountain-top.*
Hófr *hoof.*
Hólmr *island.*
Hreppr *parish.*
Hringr *ring.*
Hrútr *ram.*
Hundr *dog.*
Hungr *hunger.*
Hvelpr *whelp.*
Hverr *warm spring.*
Kálfr *calf.*
Kettlingr *kitten.*
Klettr *cliff.*
Knappr *button.*
Knífr *knife.*
Knútr *knot.*
Kólfr *arrow.*
Konungr *king.*
Koppr *cup.*
Krákr *raven.*
Krókr *hook.*
Kryplingr *cripple.*
Laukr *leek.*
Leikr *game.*
Liðr *joint.*
Ljóstr *eel-spear.*
Lokkr *lock of hair.*
Luðr *trumpet.*
Mágr *brother-in-law.*
Málmr *metal.*
Munnr *mouth.*
Naddr *spike.*
Ormr *snake, worm.*
Ostr *cheese.*
Pantr *pledge.*
Penningr *money.*
Plógr *plough.*
Pottr *pot.*
Prestr *priest.*
Pungr *purse.*
Raptr *rafter.*
Refr *fox.*
Reyrr *reed.*
Rokkr *spinning-wheel.*
Rúgr *rye.*
Salr *hall.*
Sandr *sand.*
Saumr *seam.*
Saurr *muck.*
Selr *seal.*
Skattr *treasure.*
Spikr *spike.*
Stakkr *stack.*
Stallr *stall.*
Stigr *path.*
Stokkr *stick.*
Stormr *storm.*
Straumr *stream.*
Súgr *sough (of wind).*
Taumr *rein.*
Tindr *peak.*
Toppr *top.*
Úfr *spike.*
Úlfr *wolf.*
Vágr *bay.*
Vargr *wolf.*
Víkingr *pirate.*
Vindr *wind.*
Þollr *thole (of oars).*

Some of the above nouns terminate in the *plur. nom.* in *-ar* or *-ir* indifferently.

Like *hamarr* are declined

Akr *field*.	Hafr *buck*.	Otr *otter*.	Sigr *victory*.
Aldr *age*.			

Like *þyrnir*

Einir *juniper-tree*.	Lèttir *lightness*.	Reynir *rowan-tree*.
Elrir *elder-tree*.	Læknir *physician*.	Skelmir *rogue*.
Hellir *mountain-cave*.	Missir *loss*.	Viðir *osier-twigs*.
Hersir *baron*.		

Like *hvalr*

Dalr *dale*.	Hagr *condition*.	Stafr *staff*.

Like *engill* are inflected

Áll *eel*.	Jarl *earl*.	Stöðull *milking-place*.
Biðill *wooer*.	Jökull *ice-berg*.	Söðull *saddle*.
Djöfull *devil*.	Karl *fellow*.	Virgill *or* -all *-halter*.
Dregill *strap*.	Kyrtill *kirtle*.	Vöndull *bundle*.
Fifill *dandelion*.	Skutill *spear*.	Þistill *thistle*.
Fugl *bird*.	Spegill *mirror*.	Þræll *thrall*.
Hasl *hazel*.	Stóll *seat*.	Þumall *thumb*.
Hæll *heel*.	Stuðill *prop*.	Öngull *angle*.
Igull *hedgehog*.		

Some of the above nouns, which are monosyllabic, take no *i* in the dative, particularly those in *ll*, except when they stand alone, or occupy an important place in the sentence.

Like *sveinn* are declined

Botn *ground*.	Hrafn *raven*.	Stafn *prow*.	Svefn *sleep*.
Daun *stench*.	Hreinn *reindeer*.	Steinn *stone*.	Vagn *wain*.
Dúnn *down*.	Ofn *oven*.		

Like *báss*

Áss *ridge*, *ace*.	Háls *neck*.	Íss *ice*.
Fors *or* foss *waterfall*.	Hnauss *clod*.	Óss *river's mouth*.

Griss *pig* takes *-ir* in the *plur. nom.*

Nouns whose sing. nom. ends in *-r* and plur. nom. in *-ir*;

Alr *awl*.	Hvinr *shrill sound*.	Seiðr *sorcery*.
Dynr *din*.	Kveikr *candle-wick*.	Skellr *clatter*.
Gestr *guest*.	Limr *limb*.	Skítr *dung*.
Gripr *jewel*.	Lýðr *people*.	Smiðr *smith*.
Hamr *shape*.	Rafr *halibut*.	Stafr *staff*.
Hugr *mind*.	Ságr *pail*.	Svanr *swan*.

Some substantives which do not take *r* in the nominative singular, as þjónn *servant*, are alike in the nominative and accusative singular, as well as those in *r*, *s* after a diphthong, as leir *clay*, hnauss *clod of earth*. Dissyllabic nouns, which have a simple vowel in their final syllable, are contracted in cases whose inflection begins with a vowel; as,

lykill *key.*	jötunn *giant.*	drottinn *lord.*	morgun *morn.*	aptann *eve.*
dat. lykli	jötni	drottni	*or* morni.	aptni
plur. lyklar	jötnar	drottnar		aptnar.

Some nouns which form the plural in *-ir*, insert *j* before the inflections which begin with a vowel; but this *j* before *i* is expressed by a long *i*, as hylr *abyss*, *plur.* hylír, *gen.* hylja, *dat.* hyljum, acc. hylí. After *g* and *k* the accent is omitted, as drengr *boy*, *plur.* drengir, drengja, drengjum, drengi; sekkr *sack*, *plur.* sekkir, sekkja, sękkjum, sekki.

SECOND DECLENSION.

All masculine nouns which end in *-r* or *-n* in the nominative, and in *-ar* in the genitive singular, are of this declension.

SING. *nom.* root		PLUR.	*nom.*	-ir
gen. -ar			*gen.*	-a
dat. -i			*dat.*	-um
acc. root.			*acc.*	-u.

Paradigms: siðr, hryggr, háttr, vǒllr, kjǒlr.

SINGULAR.

	A custom.	*A back.*	*A mode.*	*A valley.*	*A keel.*
N.	siðr	hryggr	háttr	vǒllr	kjǒlr
G.	siðar	hryggjar	háttar	vallar	kjalar
D.	siði	hryggi	hátti	velli	kili
A.	sið	hrygg	hátt	vǒll	kjǒl

PLURAL.

N.	siðir	hryggir	hættir	vellir	kilir
G.	siða	hryggja	hátta	valla	kjala
D.	siðum	hryggjum	háttum	vǒllum	kjǒlum
A.	siðu	hryggju	háttu	vǒllu	kjǒlu.

Like *siðr* are inflected

Burðr *burden.*	Kvistr *branch.*	Matr *meat.*	Viðr *wood.*
Feldr *cloak.*	*Liðr *joint.*	Sauðr *sheep.*	Vinr *friend.*
*Hugr *mind.*	Litr *colour.*	Staðr *stead.*	

Like *hryggr* are declined

*Beðr *bed.*	Byrr *fair wind.*	Drykkr *drink.*
*Bekkr *brook.*	Bœr *farm.*	*Elgr *elk.*

Friðr *peace.*	* Stekkr *sheep-pen.*	Veggr *wall.*
Reykr *smoke.*	Sylgr *gulp.*	Verkr *pain.*
Sekkr *sack.*	Vefr *web.*	* Vængr *wing.*

Those nouns which are marked with an asterisk take also *-s* in the *gen. sing.*

Like *háttr*

Dráttr *drawing.*	Sláttr *mowing.*	þráðr *thread.*
Máttr *might.*	þáttr *episode.*	

Like *völlr* are declined

Böllr *ball.*	Köttr *cat.*	Vöndr *wand.*
Börkr *bark.*	Mölr *moth.*	Vörðr *ward.*
Göltr *hog.*	Svörð *sword.*	Þröstr *thrush.*
Knörr *trading-vessel.*		

Like *kjölr*

Fjörðr *frith.*	Hjört *hart.*	Mjöðr *mead.*	Skjöldr *shield.*

Nouns which are without the masculine sign of *-r* in the nominative singular, remain the same in the nominative and accusative of that number, as:

SINGULAR.

	A bear.	*An eagle.*
N.	björn	örn
G.	bjarnar	arnar
D.	birni	erni
A.	björn	örn

PLURAL.

N.	birnir	ernir
G.	bjarna	arna
D.	birnum	ernum
A.	birnu	ernu

The nominative plural is formed from the dative singular, as:

Sing. nom.	sonr *a son*	*Plur. nom.* synir *sons*
gen.	sonar *of a son*	*gen.* sona *of sons*
dat.	syni *to a son*	*dat.* sonum *to sons*
acc.	son *a son*	*acc.* sonu *sons.*

The accusative plural always ends in *-i* when this vowel does not terminate the dative singular, as:

SINGULAR.

	A poem.	*A bellows.*
N.	bragr	belgr
G.	bragar	belgjar
D.	brag	belg
A.	brag	belg

Plural.

N. bragir	belgir
G. braga	belgja
D. brögum	belgjum
A. bragi	belgi.

All derivatives in *-skapr* and *-naðr* follow the endings of *siðr* in the singular, and of *bragr* in the plural; *e. g.*, búskapr *household*, skilnaðr *separation*; but the former are rarely to be met with in the plural: the latter termination *-naðr* often undergoes a vowel-change of *u*; for instance, fögnuðr (fagnaðr) *joy*, as if a *u* were omitted before *r*, the sign of the masculine.

Third Declension.

Masculine substantives which have the nominative termination in *-i*, and that of the genitive in *-a*, are of this declension.

Sing. nom.	-i	*Plur. nom.*	-ar
gen.	-a	*gen.*	-a
dat.	-a	*dat.*	-um
acc.	-a	*acc.*	-a.

Paradigm: floti.

Singular.

A fleet.

N. floti
G. flota
D. flota
A. flota

Plural.

N. flotar
G. flota
D. flotum
A. flota.

Like *floti* are declined

Auki *addition.*
Bani (no *plur.*) *bane.*
Bauti *fallen warrior.*
Bogi *curve.*
Brúðgumi *bridegroom.*
Búi *dweller.*
Dauði *death.*
Dreki *man-of-war.*
Dropi *drop.*
Endi *end.*
Fjöldi *crowd.*
Gálgi *gallows.*
Geisli *ray.*
Goði *priest.*
Hluti *lot.*
Hosti *cough.*
Hráki *spit.*
Íkorni *squirrel.*
Knefi *fist.*
Ljóri *window.*
Logi *flame.*

Máni *moon.*
Orri *heath-cock.*
Poki *bag.*
Púki *goblin.*
Risi *giant.*
Skáli *farm-dwelling.*
Skuggi *shade.*
Sleði *sledge.*
Speni *suck.*
Steði *stithy.*
Stólpi *pillar.*
Sveiti *sweat.*
Tími *time.*
Uxi *ox.*
Yrki *workman.*
Ökli *ankle.*

Uxi takes *yxna* in the *gen. plur.*

Dissyllabic nouns, whose chief vowel is *a,* change *a* into *ö* before the termination in *n* in the *dat. plur.,* as:

Sing. nom.	andi *a spirit*		*Plur. nom.*	andar *spirits*
gen.	anda *of a spirit*		*gen.*	anda *of spirits*
dat.	anda *to a spirit*		*dat.*	öndum *to spirits*
acc.	anda *a spirit*		*acc.*	anda *spirits.*

Like *andi* are declined

Arfi *heir.*
Bakki *hill.*
Drafli *milk-cheese.*
Hali *tail.*
Hani *cock.*
Hjarni *skull.*
Jaki *ice-floe.*
Kappi *champion.*
Kjarni *kernel.*
Magi *maw.*
Nafli *navel.*
Nagli *nail.*
Skaði *scath.*
Skratti *wizard.*
Stapi *cliff.*

Masculine nouns ending in *-ingi,* and some others, which are chiefly derivative words, take *j* in their oblique cases, as:

Sing. nom.	heiðingi *a heathen*		*Plur. nom.*	heiðingjar *heathen*
gen.	heiðingja *of a heathen*		*gen.*	heiðingja *of heathen*
dat.	heiðingja *to a heathen*		*dat.*	heiðingjum *to heathen*
acc.	heiðingja *a heathen*		*acc.*	heidingja *heathen.*

In the same way are declined

Frelsingi *freedman.*
Höfðingi *chieftain.*
Leysingi *freedman.*
Ræningi *robber.*
Eyskeggi *islander.*
Illvirki *evil-doer.*
Vilji *will.*

Participial substantives in *-andi* deviate only in the plural, and are inflected with *r, a, um, r,* where *r* properly stands for *ir,* and produces a vowel-change, as:

Sing. nom.	elskandi *a lover*		*Plur. nom.*	elskendr *lovers*
gen.	elskanda *of a lover*		*gen.*	elskenda (-anda) *of lovers*
dat.	elskanda *to a lover*		*dat.*	elskendum (-öndum) *to lovers*
acc.	elskanda *a lover*		*acc.*	elskendr *lovers.*

Thus are inflected

Dómandi *judge.*
Eigandi *owner.*
Hallandi *slope.*
Lesandi *reader.*
Sjáandi *eye-witness.*
Sœkjandi *suer.*
Verjandi *warder.*

Trisyllabic nouns, which have *a* in the antepenultimate and the penultimate, change the first into *ö*, and the second into *u* before *um* of the dative plural as, bakari *baker, dat. plur.* bökurum. When *a* occurs in the penultimate only, it is changed into *ö* as, fèlagi *fellow, dat. plur.* fèlögum, or into *u* as, leikari *juggler, dat. plur.* leikurum. All present participles active are declined like *elskandi* when they are used substantively: they are mostly found in the plural. Even those which have a neuter signification are masculine, if they possess this form, and take the inflections proper to that gender under this declension; they are seldom used otherwise than in the singular as, talandi *gift of speech*.

Fourth Declension.

This declension includes all feminine nouns with nominative and genitive terminations in *-a* and *u* respectively.

Sing. nom.	-a	*Plur. nom.*	-ur
gen.	-u	*gen.*	-na
dat.	-u	*dat.*	-um
acc.	-u	*acc.*	-ur.

Paradigms: tunga, gata, lína, bylgja.

Singular.

	A tongue.	*A path.*	*A line.*	*A billow.*
N.	tunga	gata	lína	bylgja
G.	tungu	götu	línu	bylgju
D.	tungu	götu	línu	bylgju
A.	tungu	götu	línu	bylgju

Plural.

N.	tungur	götur	línur	bylgjur
G.	tungna	gatna	lína	bylgna
D.	tungum	götum	línum	bylgjum
A.	tungur	götur	línur	bylgjur.

Like *tunga* are declined

Bytta *small tub.*	Edda *grandmother.*	Grýta *pot.*
Dimma *darkness.*	Fifa *cotton-grass.*	Heilsa *health.*
Drápa *dirge.*	Fura *fir-tree.*	Heimska *stupidity.*
Drekka *drink.*	Gáta *riddle.*	Heita *heat.*
Drífa *drift.*	Gedda *pike.*	Hella *flat-stone.*
Dúfa *dove.*	Genta *lass.*	Hespa *hasp.*
Dýna *feather-bed.*	Gríma *mask.*	Hola *cave.*

Hulda *veil.*	Köngurváfa *spider.*	Sýsla *district.*
Kápa *cloak.*	Misa *whey.*	Títa *kind of sparrow.*
Kelda *fountain.*	Mugga *mist.*	Vika *week.*
Kisa *puss.*	Næpa *turnip.*	Vísa *verse.*
Kista *chest.*	Pika *girl.*	Væta *wet.*
Kráka *crow.*	Skreppa *wallet.*	Þoka *fog.*
Kringla *circle.*	Skriða *slip (as of snow).*	Þúfa *knoll.*
Krukka *jar.*		

Like *gata*

Aska *ashes.*	Hlaða *barn.*	Sala *sale.*
Bjalla *bell.*	Kaka *thin cake.*	Stjarna *star.*
Blanda *mixture.*	Kanna *can.*	Tala *speech.*
Haka *hook.*	Naðra *viper.*	Vagga *cradle.*
Harpa *harp.*	Saga *story.*	

Like *lína* are inflected skepna *creature,* and tinna *flint.*

These below are like *bylgja* in their inflections.

Bryggja *pier.*	Fylgja *tutelary spirit.*	Skeggja *axe.*
Ekkja *widow.*	Kirkja *church.*	Skyggja *mirror.*
Eskja *ash.*	Rekkja *bed.*	Þykkja *thought.*

Nouns ending in *-ja* where *g* or *k* does not precede, do not take *n* in the *gen. plur.*, as: brynja *cuirass*, ferja *ferry,* lilja *lily,* smiðja *smithy,* which are the same in the *gen. plur.* as the *nom. sing.*

Some nouns of this declension are used chiefly in the plural as, átölur *upbraidings*, gætur *care, attention,* líkur *likeness,* fortölur *persuasion.* Brenna *burning,* vera *being,* and other infinitives in *a,* used substantively, are of this declension.

Fifth Declension.

Feminine nouns which have various terminations in the nominative singular, and which end in *-ar* or *-ir* in the nominative plural, are of this declension.

Sing. nom.	root	*Plur. nom.*	-ar, -ir
gen.	-ar	*gen.*	-a
dat.	root, -u, *or* -i	*dat.*	-um
acc.	root, -i	*acc.*	-ar, -ir.

Paradigms: eign, brúðr, vör, drottning, egg, ör, heiði, á, andvarpan, fjöður, alin.

Singular.

	A property.	*A bride.*	*A lip.*
N.	eign	brúðr	vör
G.	eignar	brúðar	varar
D.	eign	brúði	vör
A.	eign	brúði	vör

Plural.

N.	eignir	brúðir	varir
G.	eigna	brúða	vara
D.	eignum	brúðum	vörum
A.	eignir	brúðir	varir.

Like *eign* are declined

Alpt *swan.*
Ambátt *female slave.*
Ást *love.*
Auðn *desert.*
Baun *bean.*
Borg *fortress.*
Breidd *breadth.*
Búð *booth.*
Byggð *settlement.*
Byrðr *burden.*
Dáð *deed.*
Dís *goddess.*
Ferð *journey.*
Gaupn *fist.*
Gipt *gift.*
Grein *branch.*
Grund *ground.*
Hjálm *helm.*
Hjálp *help.*
Húð *hide.*
Lausn *redemption.*
Leið *way.*
Lind *linden-tree.*
Lind *fountain.*
Pinsl *torture.*
Seil *rope.*
Sjón *sight.*
Skál *bowl.*
Skeið *spoon.*
Skírn *baptism.*
Skuld *debt.*
Sókn *parish.*
Sorg *sorrow.*
Sótt *sickness.*
Stund *hour.*
Tíð *time.*
Tíund *tithe.*
Tryggð *surety.*
Váð *cloth.*
Vág *weight.*
Ván *hope.*
Vist *food.*
Þjóð *people.*

From the above examples it will be seen that when neither *a* nor *ö* constitutes the root-vowel, no modification takes place.

Like *vör* are declined

Björk *birch.*
Gjörðr *girth.*
Hjörð *herd.*
Höfn *haven.*
Höll *hall.*
Jörð *earth.*
Skömm *shame.*
Sögn *saying.*
Sök cause.
Vömb *womb.*
Vörn *defence.*
Þökk *thanks.*
Ögn *chaff.*
Örð *ploughing.*
Öx *axe.*
Öxl *shoulder.*

No substantive under this declension has uniformly preserved the *u* of the dative singular, except a few which insert *j* or *v*, and all in *ing* and *ung*, and even in these it is sometimes dropt. The *nom.* and *acc. plur.* termination *-ar* is used in all derivatives in *ing* and *ung* as, drottning *queen,* hörmung *woe*, and in all those primitives which insert *j* or *v* as, mey *maid,* ör *arrow,* as well as in monosyllables ending in a vowel: however, practice only can determine which substantives of this declension take *ar* or *ir* in those cases.

SINGULAR.

	A queen.	A ridge.	An arrow.	A heath.	A river.
N.	drottning	egg	ör	heiði	á
G.	drottningar	eggjar	örvar	heiðar	ár
D.	drottningu	egg	öru	heiði	á
A.	drottning	egg	ör	heiði	á

PLURAL.

N.	drottningar	eggjar	örvar	heiðar	ár
G.	drottninga	eggja	örva	heiða	áa
D.	drottningum	eggjum	örum	heiðum	ám
A.	drottningar	eggjar	örvar	heiðar	ár.

Like *drottning* are declined

Djörfúng *boldness.* | Hyrníng *corner.* | Messíng (*no pl.*) *brass.*
Eldíng *kindling.* | Hörmúng *misery.* | Siglíng *sailing.*

Like *egg* are declined

Ben *wound.*
Eng *meadow.*
Ey *island.*
Hel (*dat.*-ju) *abode of death.*
Il *sole of the foot.*
Klyf *bundle.*
Mey *maid.*
Nyt *gain.*
Þy *she-thrall.*

Like *ör*

Dögg *dew.* | Stöð *place.* | Þröng *crowd.*

Like *heiði*

Ermi *sleeve.*
Eyri *low sandy shore.*
Festi *rope.*
Herðr *shoulder.*
Hlið *side.*
Laug *bath.*
Myri *moor.*
Nál *needle.*
Sin *sinew.*

Like *á* are declined

Brá *brow.*
Gjá *chasm.*
Rá *roe.*
Skrá *parchment.*
Spá *prophecy.*
Vá *damage.*
Þá *thaw.*

Nouns of more than one syllable having the nominative ending of *-ul* or *ur,* are contracted before the inflections which begin with a vowel as, göndul *amazon,* fjöður *feather.* Derivatives in *an* have also another form in *un,* both of which are regular.

SINGULAR.

	A sigh.	A feather.	An ell.
N.	andvarpan *or* -vörpun	fjöður	alin
G.	andvarpanar *or* -vörpunar	fjaðrar	álnar
D.	andvarpan *or* -vörpun	fjöður	alin
A.	andvarpan *or* -vörpun	fjöður	alin

PLURAL.

N.	andvarpanir	fjaðrir	álnir
G.	andvarpana	fjaðra	álna
D.	andvörpunum	fjöðrum	álnum
A.	andvarpanir	fjaðrir	álnir.

Andvarpan is derived from andi *breath,* and verpa *to cast* or *send forth.*

Like this noun are declined dýrkan *cultivation,* and skemtan *or* skemtun *amusement.*

A few of those substantives which insert *j* are used only in the plural as, menjar *tokens, signs.*

Some nouns in *i* form their nominative and accusative plural in *ir* as, gleði *cheerfulness,* elli *age,* and do not take *ar* in the genitive singular, but are indeclinable throughout that number.

SIXTH DECLENSION.

Feminine nouns, whose nominative plural ends in *r,* follow this declension.

Sing. nom.	root	*Plur. nom.*	-r
gen.	-ar, -r	*gen.*	-a
dat.	root	*dat.*	-um
acc.	root	*acc.*	-r.

Paradigms: grind, tönn, bót, mörk, spöng.

SINGULAR.

A grate.	*A tooth.*	*A fine.*	*A wood.*	*A clasp.*
N. grind	tönn	bót	mörk	spöng
G. grindar	tannar	bótar	merkr, markar	spengr, spangar
D. grind	tönn	bót	mörk	spöng
A. grind	tönn	bót	mörk	spöng

PLURAL.

N. grindr	tennr	bætr	merkr, markir	spengr, spangir
G. grinda	tanna	bóta	marka	spanga
D. grindum	tönnum	bótum	mörkum	spöngum
A. grindr	tennr	bætr	merkr, markir	spengr, spangir.

Like *grind* are declined

Ert *pea.* | Geit *she-goat.* | Hind *hind.* | Kinn *cheek.*

Like *tönn*

Strönd *strand.* | Önd *duck.* | Ört *teal.*

Like *bót*

Glóð *embers*. | Hnot *nut*. | Rót root.

Like *mörk*

Eik *oak*. | Mjólk *milk*. | Steik *steak*. | Vík *small bay*.

Like *spöng*

Röng *timbers of a ship*. | Stöng *pole*. | Sæng *bed*. | Töng *sea-weed*.

As will be seen in the last two paradigms (mörk *and* spöng), nouns of this declension which terminate in *g* or *k*, commonly form the genitive singular in *r*, like the nominative plural: bók *book*, on the other hand, always has the genitive bókar, *plur*. bækr.

Those substantives whose nominative singular is *d* or *t*, mostly have the genitive in *-ar*, as strönd, *gen*. strandar, rót, *gen*. rótar, whilst those in *g* or *k* usually form the genitive in the same way as the nominative plural, as stöng, *gen. sing*. and *nom. plur*. stengr, mörk, *gen. sing*. and *nom. plur*. merkr. Most nouns in this declension which have *ó* in the root-syllable, can also follow the fifth declension.

Nouns which terminate in a vowel are declined like bót, for instance, ló *plover*, *gen*. lóar, *plur*. lœr, lóm, lóa; such are

Brú	(*gen*. brúar. *plur*. brýr *or* brúr)	*bridge*.
Fló	» » » flar » »	*flea*.
Frú	(*gen. sing*. and *nom. plur*. frúr)	*woman*.
Há	» » » » » »	*hide*.
Kló	» » » » » »	*claw*.
Krá	» » » » » »	*corner*.
Ljá	» » » » » »	*newly mown grass*.
Ró	(no *plur*.)	*iron-plate*.
Tá	(*gen. sing*. tár)	*toe*.
Trú	(no *plur*.)	*faith*.
Þró	» »	*a kind of box*.

SEVENTH DECLENSION.

All neuter nouns which have the nominative-ending *-a* are of this declension.

Sing. nom.	-a	*Plur. nom.*	-u
gen.	-a	*gen.*	-na
dat.	-a	*dat.*	-um
acc.	-a	*acc.*	-u.

Paradigms: eyra, hjarta.

SINGULAR.

	An ear.	*A heart.*
N.	eyra	hjarta
G.	eyra	hjarta
D.	eyra	hjarta
A.	eyra	hjarta

PLURAL.

N.	eyru	hjörtu
G.	eyrna	hjörtna
D.	eyrum	hjörtum
A.	eyru	hjörtu.

The radical *a* of the noun is changed into *ö* before inflections in *u,* as in the above example.

Like *eyra* are declined

Auga *eye.*	Hnoða *key.*	Nýra *kidney.*
Bjúga *sausage.*	Lunga *lung.*	

Eighth Declension.

Monosyllabic neuter nouns, and those of this gender that end in consonants, or in *-i,* have the following inflections:

Sing. nom.	root	*Plur. nom.*	root
gen.	-s	*gen.*	-a
dat.	-i	*dat.*	-um
acc.	root	*acc.*	root.

Paradigms: orð, barn, sumar, höfuð, kvæði, knè, kyn, ríki, söl.

SINGULAR.

	A word.	*A child.*	*A summer.*	*A head.*
N.	orð	barn	sumar	höfuð
G.	orðs	barns	sumars	höfuðs
D.	orði	barni	sumri	höfði
A.	orð	barn	sumar	höfuð

PLURAL.

N.	orð	börn	sumur	höfuð
G.	orða	barna	sumra	höfða
D.	orðum	börnum	sumrum	höfðum
A.	orð	börn	sumur	höfuð.

Only in those nouns whose terminating syllable begins with a vowel does contraction take place, as in the last two examples: this likewise applies to the other declensions.

Like *orð* are declined

Ár *year.*
Bál *funeral pile.*
Bein *leg.*
Bik *pitch.*
Blek *ink.*
Blik *splendour.*
Blóð *blood.*
Blóm *flower.*
Blót *sacrifice.*
Bly *lead.*
Blys *torch.*
Boð *offer.*
Ból *farm.*
Borð *board, table.*
Brauð *bread.*
Brèf *letter.*
Brjóst *breast.*
Brúðkaup *wedding.*
Bú *farm.*
Bygg *barley.*
Deig *dough.*
Dikt *poem.*
Djúp *depth.*
Dráp *murder.*
Drep *battle.*
Drif *drift.*
Dupt *dust.*
Dust *do.*
Dýr *animal.*
Eir *copper.*
Eik *venom.*
El *shower.*
Fen *marsh.*
Fjós *stall for cattle.*
Fóðr *fodder.*
Fólk *folk.*
Fóstr *maintenance.*
Frost *frost.*
Garn *yarn.*
Gólfr *floor.*
Grjót *stone.*
Gull *gold.*
Hár *hair.*
Haust *autumn.*
Hesl *hazel-tree.*
Hjól *wheel.*
Hlaup *leap.*
Hljóð *sound.*
Hof *heathen temple.*
Holt *wooded height.*
Hopp *leap.*
Horn *horn.*
Hraun *lava.*
Hrím *hoar-frost.*
Hrogn *spawn.*
Hross *steed.*
Hús *house.*
Husl *housel* (*sacrament*).
Hvísl *whistling.*
Járn *iron.*
Jól *Christmas.*
Kál *cabbage.*
Kaup *purchase.*
Kið *kid.*
Kitl *tickling.*
Kjöt *flesh.*
Klif *cliff.*
Korn *corn.*
Kot *cottage.*
Kvöld *evening.*
Lán *loan.*
Lauf *leaf.*
Leðr *leather.*
Leir *clay.*
Líf *life.*
Lík *corpse.*
Lím *lime.*
Lín *flax.*
Ljós *light.*
Log *flame.*
Lopt *air.*
Lær *thigh.*
Mál *measure, speech.*
Morð *murder.*
Mý *gnat.*
Net *net.*
Ok *yoke.*
Ráð *advice.*
Regn *rain.*
Reip *rope.*
Rúm *room.*
Ryk *dust.*
Sáð *seed.*
Salt *salt.*
Sár *wound.*
Segl *sail.*
Silfr *silver.*
Sinn *time.*
Skáld *poet.*
Skaut *shirt.*
Skin *sheen.*
Skip *ship.*
Skrín *shrine.*
Skúm *darkness.*
Slit *rent.*
Spjót *spear.*
Stál *steel.*
Stí *path.*
Stig *steep.*
Stríð *strife.*
Sund *sound.*
Sverð *sword*
Svín *swine.*
Tár *tear.*
Tin *tin.*
Trog *trough.*
Tröll *ogre.*
Tún *enclosure.*
Vápn *weapon.*
Vár *spring.*
Þing *council.*

Like *barn* are declined

Afl *strength.*
Agn *bait.*
Ax *ear of corn.*
Bak *back.*
Band *bandage.*
Bann *ban.*
Bjarg *mountain.*
Blað *leaf.*
Fang *grasp.*
Far *journey.*
Fax *mane.*
Fjall *mountain.*
Gafl *gable.*
Gagn *profit.*
Gap *opening.*
Gjald *payment.*
Gras *grass.*
Haf *sea.*

Happ *luck.*	Sax *short sword.*	Tal *speech.*
Lamb *lamb.*	Skap *shape.*	Tjald *tent.*
Land *land.*	Skapt *shaft.*	Val *choice.*
Nafn *name.*	Skarð *sherd.*	Vatn *water.*
Nagl *nail.*		

Neuter nouns of more than one syllable terminating in *að, al* or *an* are not contracted, with the exception of gaman *joke,* as, hèrað *district,* óðal *property,* mannlikan *image of human shape.*

Substantives in *i* do not admit another *i* in the dative as,

Sing. nom.	kvæði *a song.*	*Plur. nom.*	kvæði *songs*
gen.	kvæðis *of a song*	*gen.*	kvæða *of songs*
dat.	kvæði *to a song*	*dat.*	kvæðum *to songs*
acc.	kvæði *a song*	*acc.*	kvæði *songs.*

Thus are declined

Belti *belt.*	Fylki *district.*	Hveiti *wheat.*
Enni *forehead.*	Gerði *hedge.*	Keili *wedge.*
Eski *ash-tree.*	Gildi *banquet.*	Klæði *clothes.*
Eyði *desert.*	Herfi *harrow.*	Skæri *shears.*
Fidrildi *butterfly.*	Hlægi *laughter.*	

In some nouns of this declension *j* or *v* is inserted before the oblique cases which begin with a vowel, but never *j* before *i,* and seldom *v* before *u.* Thus

SINGULAR.

	A knee.	*A lineage.*
N.	knè	kyn
G.	knès	kyns
D.	knè	kyni
A.	knè	kyn

PLURAL.

N.	knè	kyn
G.	knjá	kynja
D.	knjám	kynjum
A.	knè	kyn.

Like *knè* are declined

Hlè *lee.* | Klè *loom-weight.* | Spè *joke.* | Trè *tree.*

Like *kyn*

Gey *barking.* | Grey *hound.* | Hey *hay.* | Nes *cape.*

Substantives, whose root-letter is *g* or *k,* admit of *j* before the inflections *a* and *um*, as well as nouns with consonantal endings which have simple vowels as,

Sing. nom. ríki *a kingdom*		*Plur. nom.* ríki *kingdoms*	
gen. ríkis *of a kingdom*		*gen.* ríkja *of kingdoms*	
dat. ríki *to a kingdom*		*dat.* ríkjum *to kingdoms*	
acc. ríki *a kingdom.*		*acc.* ríki *kingdoms.*	

Thus are declined

Ber *berry.*	Ker *drinking-cup.*	Rif *rib.*
Egg *egg.*	Klif *cliff.*	Skegg *beard.*
Gil *cleft.*	Nef *nose.*	Stef *burden (of a song).*

Some nouns with the diphthongal vowel *ö*, insert *v* before the inflections which begin with a vowel, as:

Sing. nom. söl *a seaweed*	*Plur. nom.* söl *seaweeds*
gen. söls *of a seaweed*	*gen.* sölva *of seaweeds*
dat. sölvi *to a seaweed*	*dat.* sölum *to seaweeds*
acc. söl *a seaweed.*	*acc.* söl *seaweeds.*

Thus are declined

Fjör *life-strength.* | Mjöl *meal.* | Smjör *butter.* | Öl *ale.*

Frjó *or* fræ *seed*, hræ *corpse*, and læ *deceit*, are similarly inflected.

The noun fræði *knowledge* is feminine in the singular number, and is indeclinable like æfi *life;* but in the plural it is neuter, and is declined like kvæði.

Some nouns of this declension occur both with and without the nominative-ending *-i* as;

eng *or* engi *meadow*, fullting *or* fulltingi *help*, rensl *or* rensli *drain*, sinn *or* sinni *time.*

ANOMALOUS NOUNS.

FIRST DECLENSION.

SINGULAR.

God.	*A blast.*	*A day.*	*A chip.*	*An ounce.*	*A kettle.*
N. Guð	blást-r	dag-r	spánn *or* spónn	eyrir	ketil-l
G. —s	——ar, -rar, -rs	——s	spánns	—-is	——s
D. —i	blæsti	degi	spæni	—i	katli
A. Guð	blást	dag	spánn	—i	ketil

PLURAL.

N.	Guðir, -ar	blástar, -rar	dagar	spænir	aur-ar	katlar
G.	—a	——a	—a	spána	——a	—la
D.	—um	——um	dögum	——um	——um	kötlum
A.	—ir, -ar	——a	daga	——a	——a	katla.

SINGULAR.

	A shoe.	*A man.*	*A finger.*
N.	skó-r	maðr	fing-r
G.	——s	manns	——rs, -rar
D.	——	——i	——ri
A.	——	——	——r

PLURAL.

N.	skó-r, skú-ar	menn	fing-rar
G.	——a, ——a	manna	——ra
D.	——m	mönnum	——rum
A.	——, ——a	menn	——rar.

SECOND DECLENSION.

SINGULAR.

	A wind.	*A way.*	*Snow.*	*A foot.*
N.	vind-r	veg-r	snær, snjár, snjór	fót-r
G.	——s, -ar	——ar, -s	snævar, snjávar, snjóar, snjós	—ar
D.	——i	——i	snævi, snæ, snjá, snjó, snjóvi	fœti
A.	——	——	snæ, snjá, snjó	fót

PLURAL.

N.	——ar	—ar, -ir	snævar, snjávar, snjóar, snjóvar	fœtr
G.	——a	—a	snæva, snjáva, snjóa	fóta
D.	——um	—um	snævum, snjávum, snjám, snjáum, snjóum	—um
A.	——a	—a	snæva, snjáva, snjóa	fœtr.

SINGULAR.

	A father.	*A brother.*	*Winter.*
N.	faðir	bróð-ir	vetr
G.	feðr, föður, föðrs	——ur, bræðr, bróðurs	—ar
D.	föður	——	—i
A.	——	——	——

PLURAL.

N.	feðr	bræðr	vetr, -ar
G.	—a	——a	—a
D.	—um	——um	—um
A.	——	——	—, -ar.

Like *vindr* are declined skógr *a wood,* grautr *groats,* and some other words which follow the inflections of *síðr* (2nd declension) in the singular, and of *hestr* (1st declension) in the plural.

Sær *sea* is declined like *snær*, and móðir *mother,* dóttir *daughter,* are inflected like *bróðir.* Systir *sister* is declined as follows:

Sing. nom.	systir	*Plur. nom.*	systr
gen.	systur	*gen.*	——a
dat.	——	*dat.*	systr-um
acc.	——	*acc.*	——

THIRD DECLENSION.

SINGULAR.

	A yeoman.	*A fiend, foe.*
N.	bóndi *contracted for* bóandi, búandi	fjandi *contr. for* fjáandi
G.	bónda	fjanda
D.	bónda	fjanda
A.	bónda	fjanda

PLURAL.

N.	bóndr, bœndr	fjandr, fjendr
G.	bónda, bœnda, bóanda, búanda, búenda	fjanda
D.	bóndum	fjandum
A.	bœndr	fjandr, fjendr.

FOURTH DECLENSION.

SINGULAR.

	A woman.	*A prophetess.*
N.	kon-a, kun-a	val-a, völ-va
G.	——u	völ-u, ——vu
D.	——	——, ——
A.	——	——, ——

PLURAL.

N.	——ur	——r, ——r
G.	kvenna, kvinna	——na
D.	kon-um	——um
A.	——ur	——r.

FIFTH DECLENSION.

Sál *soul* is thus declined:

Sing. nom.	sál, sál-a	*Plur. nom.*	sál-ir, sál-ur
gen.	—ar, —u	*gen.*	—na, —na
dat.	—u, —	*dat.*	—um, —um
acc.	—, —	*acc.*	—ir. —ur.

SIXTH DECLENSION.

SINGULAR.

	A hand.	*Night.*	*A cow.*	*An ewe.*	*An eyebrow.*
N.	hönd	nátt, nótt	kýr	ær	brún
G.	handar	nátt-ar, nætr	kýr	ær	brún-ar
D.	hendi	——	kú	á	——
A.	hönd	——	—	—	——

PLURAL.

N.	hendr	nætr	kýr	ær	brýnn, brýn, brýr
G.	handa	nátt-a, nótta	kúa	á	brún-a
D.	höndum	——um,	—m	—m	——um
A.	hendr	nætr	kýr	ær	brýnn, brýn, brýr.

SINGULAR.

	A goose.	*A mouse.*
N.	gás, gæs	mús
G.	—-ar	——ar
D.	—	——
A.	—-	——-

PLURAL.

			A door. fem.	neut.
N.	gæss	mýss	dyrr	dyr
G.	gás-a	mús-a	dur-a	—a
D.	——um	——um	——um	—-um
A.	gæss	mýss	dyrr	—-

Like *mús* is declined lús *a louse.*

EIGHTH DECLENSION.

SINGULAR.

	Cattle.	*A temple.*
N.	fè	vè
G.	fjár	—s
D.	fè	—
A.	—	—

PLURAL.

			Sound.	*The gods.*
N.	—	—	læti	regin, rögn
G.	fjá	—a	lát-a	ragna
D.	—m	—um	—um	rögnum
A.	fè	—	læti	regin, rögn.

A few neuter nouns change their gender to the feminine in the plural number, as:

SINGULAR.	PLURAL.
lim *twig*	limar *boughs.*
mund *time*	mundir *times.*
tál *fraud*	tálar *frauds.*

Some names of relatives, with different terminations, which include two or more persons in one name, are consequently used only in the plural: if the two persons are of different genders they take the neuter:

hjón *man and woman, married people;*
systkin *brother and sister;*
feðgin *father and daughter;*
mœðgin *mother and son;*
feðgar *father and son;*
mœðgur *mother and daughter.*

DECLENSION OF NOUNS WITH THE ARTICLE.

An example in each declension of a noun with the article appended, appears as follows:

FIRST DECLENSION. *The horse.*		FIFTH DECLENS. *The property.*	
Sing.	Plur.	Sing.	Plur.
N. hestr-inn	*N.* hestar-nir	*N.* eign-in	*N.* eignar-nar
G. hests-ins	*G.* hesta-nna	*G.* eignar-innar	*G.* eigna-nna
D. hesti-num	*D.* hestu-num	*D.* eign-inni	*D.* eignu-num
A. hest-inn	*A.* hesta-na	*A.* eign-ina	*A.* eignir-nar

SECOND DECLENS. *The custom.*		SIXTH DECLENSION. *The grate.*	
Sing.	Plur.	Sing.	Plur.
N. siðr-inn	*N.* siðir-nir	*N.* grind-in	*N.* grindr-nar
G. siðar-ins	*G.* siða-nna	*G.* grindar-innar	*G.* grinda-nna
D. siði-num	*D.* siðu-num	*D.* grind-inni	*D.* grindu-num
A. sið-inn	*A.* siðu-na	*A.* grind-ina	*A.* grindr-nar

THIRD DECLENSION. *The fleet.*		SEVENTH DECLENSION. *The ear.*	
Sing.	Plur.	Sing.	Plur.
N. floti-nn	*N.* flotar-nir	*N.* eyra-t	*N.* eyru-n
G. flota-ns	*G.* flota-nna	*G.* eyra-ns	*G.* eyrna-nna
D. flota-num	*D.* flotu-num	*D.* eyra-nu	*D.* eyru-num
A. flota-nn	*A.* flota-na	*A.* eyra-t	*A.* eyru-n

FOURTH DECLENS. *The tongue.*		EIGHTH DECLENSION. *The word.*	
Sing.	Plur.	Sing.	Plur.
N. tunga-n	*N.* tungur-nar	*N.* orð-it	*N.* orð-in
G. tungu-nnar	*G.* tungna-nna	*G.* orðs-ins	*G.* orða-nna
D. tungu-nni	*D.* tungu-num	*D.* orði-nu	*D.* orðu-num
A. tungu-na	*A.* tungur-nar	*A.* orð-it	*A.* orð-in.

The neuter *it* occurs in some books in the form *ið*, especially after a radical *t;* and in all cases of Modern Icelandic.

The aspirate *h* appears to be of later origin; the oldest manuscripts have *inn, in, it*, or even *enn, en, et*.

When three *n*-endings come together one is rejected as, brún *eyebrow*, *plur*. brýnn; with the article, *brýnnar* for *brýnn-nar*.

Maðr *man* adds to the nom. plur. *-ir* and to the acc. *-i*, thus, menn -ir -nir, menn -i -na. Faðir and bróðir insert *s* in the gen. sing., as, föðurs-ins, bróðurs-ins. After liquids *i* is dropped, as salr, hvalr, *dat. sing*. salnum, hvalnum.

Nouns which end in a diphthongic vowel reject the *i* of the article when in other cases it would make two syllables as, ey-nni, á-nni, kú-nni: in the accusative ey-na, á-na, kú-na.

The genitive singular of monosyllabic feminine substantives is generally contracted when they are declined indefinitely; but it is always lengthened when the article is appended, as: frú *woman, gen.* frúr, frúar-innar; yet á *river*, ær *ewe* and kýr *cow* are exceptions, and form ár-innar, ær--innar, and kýr-innar.

INFLECTION OF PROPER NOUNS.

1. Names of persons.

Masculines in *-r* are generally declined like *hestr*, for instance, Þórr, *gen*. Þórs, Þorgeirr, Þorgeirs. To this class belong also those in *-arr*, as, Gunnarr, Fjálarr, which in the dative take *-ari* as, Gunnari, Fjálari, not being contracted like *hamarr*.

In *-ir* as *Þyrnir, e. g.*, Hænir, Hamdir.

In *-all, -ill, -ull* like common nouns of the same termination, as, Hagalls, *gen*. Hagals, *dat*. Hagli, Reginn, Regni, Egill, Egli. Ketill in compounds mostly becomes *-kell*, and in the dative both Þorkatli and Þorkeli, Hallkatli and Hallkeli occur.

Masculines ending in *-undr, -uðr, -urðr, -viðr, -röðr, -aðr, -llr, -an, -on, -un* are inflected like *siðr*, namely, with the genitive in *-ar*, -dative *-i* as, Sigurðr, *gen*. Sigurðar, *dat*. Sigurði, Önundr, Önundar, Önundi, Arnviðar, Arnviði, Guðröðar, Guðröði, Niðaðr, Niðaðar, Niðaði, Ullr, Ullar, Ulli, Heimdallr, Heimdallar, Heimdalli, Hálfdan, Hálfdanar,

Hálfdani, Hákon, Hákonar, Hákoni, Auðun, Auðunar, Auðuni; of these as well as of appellatives in *-naðr* a form of vowel-change is sometimes found in the nominative as, Niðuðr, Heimdöllr..

Where instead of *-urðr* the original *-varðr* occurs, the gen. *-s* is chiefly used as, Hallvarðr, Hallvarðs.

All masculines in *-i* follow the third declension as, Snorri, Helgi, Atli.

Feminines in *-r, -nn* and *-dís* are inflected mostly like *brúðr* (in the 5th declension) as, Hildr, Gerðr and all derivatives therefrom;

N.	Auðr	Unnr *or* Uðr	Sigriðr	Jórun	Hjördís
G.	Auðar	Unnar	Sigriðar	Jórunar	Hjördísar
D.	Auði	Unni	Sigriði	Jóruni	Hjördísi
A.	Auði	Unni	Sigriði	Jóruni	Hjördísi.

All those ending in -dís are declined in the same manner, although the word *dís* itself has its cases like *eign*.

Many polysyllabic feminines have the genitive in *-ar*, but the dative and accusative in *-u* as,

N.	Guðrún	Signý	Óluf	Rannveig
G.	———ar	——jar	——ar	————ar
D.	———u	——ju	——u	————u
A.	———u	——ju	——u	————u.

Monosyllabic feminines form the dative and accusative like the nominative as, Hlíf, *gen.* Hlífar, *dat.* and *acc.* Hlíf; most of these insert *j* in the genitive; Frigg, Síf, Hel, *gen.* -jar.

All feminines in *-a* follow the 4th declension as, Bera, Embla, Katla, þórhalla.

Some few names of men have a feminine form as, Sturla, Sturlu, Úrækja, Úrækju. Skaði on the other hand, which is a female name, is inflected like *floti* (3rd declension).

From the names of men those of women are chiefly formed by adding *a* to the root-form as:

masc.	Hallr	Ketill	Þorkell	Þórörn	Hrafn
fem.	Halla	Katla	Þorkatla	Þórarna	Hrefna.

When an appellative is used as a masculine proper noun, a feminine word answering to it being found, the latter is also used as a corresponding feminine name, both singly and in compounds, as:

masc.	Björn	Hallbjörn
fem.	Bera	Hallbera.

Foreign names take either a form which can be inflected according to the examples above adduced, *e. g.* Mikjáll, Mikjáls, Lafranz, *gen.* Lafranz, *dat.* Lafranzi, or retain their native form; in this case they are inflected either as Icelandic names, *e. g.* Magnús, Magnúss, *or* Magnúsar, Gregoriús, Gregoriúsar, Elías, Elíasar, Aron, Arons, or declined like Latin names as, Christophorus, Christophori, Julianus, Juliani.

2. Names of places.

Many nouns of this class are appellatives, and can therefore be inflected like common nouns as, berg, hof, staðr, völlr, heimr, fit, and compounded as Forberg, þórshof, Sólheimr. Several are used in the plural, as -staðir (Faxstaðir), -vellir (Möðruvellir), -heimar (Sólheimar), Fitjar, á Fitjum.

Some words appear no longer as appellatives, *e. g.* ló, *gen.* lóar *beach;* vin *gen.* vinjar, *plur.* vinjar *pasture;* þveit *gen.* þveitar *fragment;* but as names, for instance, Lóar, *dat.* Lóm, Vinjar, *dat.* Vinjum. In composition, deviations from the rules of inflection sometimes take place; thus many form in *Ló* are indeclinable; vin sometimes takes vinar for vinjar as, Björgvinar for Björgvinjar. When *vin* in composition immediately follows a consonant, it becomes *yn, ynar* or *ynjar:* thus Björgyn, Björgynjar, Sköðyn, Sköðynar, and in such cases the absorbed *v* effects a vowel-change, thus, Taðvin, Töðyn, Sandvin, Söndyn.

When *rjóðr* (a cleared space) is used as the name of a place, it often becomes *ruð* as, þjóstólfsruð, Ausuruð; yet the original form may be preserved as, Bernrjóðr, Hristarrjóðr.

The forms Gula, Aga, Odda, Frosta, and others are indeclinable.

Few names of places appear without the definite article as, Mær-in, Vangr-inn, Skiðan, *dat.* Skiðunni, Vellir-nir.

CHAPTER III.

OF THE ADJECTIVE.

The adjective has two forms, the indefinite as, *svartr* hestr *a black horse* or hestrinn er *svartr the horse is black,* and the definite as, hinn *svarti* hestr *the black horse*, with the usual cases in each.

1. The Positive.

The inflections are these:

INDEFINITE FORM.

	Masc.	*Fem.*	*Neut.*
Sing. nom.	-r (l, n, s)	Root (with vowel-change of *u*)	-t
gen.	-s	-rar	-s
dat.	-um	-ri	-u
acc.	-an.	-a	-t
Plur. nom.	-ir	-ar	Root (with vowel-change of *u*)
gen.	-ra	-ra	-ra
dat.	-um	-um	-um
acc.	-a	-ar	Root (with vowel-change of *u*).

DEFINITE FORM.

	Masc.	*Fem.*	*Neut.*
Sing. nom.	-i	-a	-a
gen.	-a	-u	-a
dat.	-a	-u	-a
acc.	-a	-u	-a.

The inflections in the plural are *-u*.

The definite form in the singular is thus inflected like nouns of the 3rd, 4th, and 5th declension.

Paradigm: hvatr *quick*.

INDEFINITE.

SING.

	Masc.	*Fem.*	*Neut.*
N.	hvat-r	hvöt	hvat-t
G.	hvat-s	hvat-rar	hvat-s
D.	hvöt-um	hvat-ri	hvöt-u
A.	hvat-an	hvat-a	hvat-t

PLUR.

	Masc.	*Fem.*	*Neut.*
N.	hvat-ir	hvat-ar	hvöt
G.	hvat-ra	hvat-ra	hvat-ra
D.	hvöt-um	hvöt-um	hvöt-um
A.	hvat-a	hvat-ar	hvöt

DEFINITE.

SING.

Masc.	*Fem.*	*Neut.*
hvat-i	hvat-a	hvat-a
hvat-a	hvöt-u	hvat-a
hvat-a	hvöt-u	hvat-a
hvat-a	hvöt-u	hvat-a

PLUR.

hvöt-u throughout.

Thus are declined;

gjarn *greedy.*	harðr *hard.*	krankr *ill.*	snar *swift.*
hagr *active.*	hvass *sharp.*	rangr *wrong.*	spakr *wise.*

Adjectives take the definite endings when the article is appended to the noun as, *svarti hestrinn, svarta hestinn.*

The masculine sign *-r* is lost when the root is *rr, ss, fn, gn, kn, rn,* as, þurr *dry,* hvass *sharp,* jafn *even,* skyggn *clear-sighted,* frœkn *bold,* gjarn *willing, greedy.*

The feminine form has in the nominative singular the root with *u*-vowel-change on account of the omission of *u* in the masculine termination, as, svört (from svartr *swart*), glöð (from glaðr *glad*).

The neuter form has in the nominative singular *t,* with which ð and *n* are assimilated to *tt,* for instance, goðr, gott *good,* sannr satt *true.*

Polysyllabic words in *inn,* and the adjectives mikill *much,* litill *little,* form their neuters in *it;* if the root end with a double consonant the latter is made single before *t* as, lauss laust, sæll sælt.

Paradigms: búiun *ready,* lítill *little,* lauss *loose,* sæll *happy.*

INDEFINITE.

	Sing.			Sing.	
Masc.	Fem.	Neut.	Masc.	Fem.	Neut.
N. búin-n	búin	búi-t	lítil-l	lítil	líti-t (litt)
G. búin-s	búin-nar	búin-s	lítil-s	lítil-lar	lítil-s
D. bún-um	búin-ni	bún-u	litl-um	lítil-li	litl-u
A. búin-n	bún-a	búi-t	lítin-n	litl-a	líti-t (litt)
	Plur.			Plur.	
N. bún-ir	bún-a	búin	litl-ir	litl-ar	lítil
G. búin-na	búin-na	búin-na	lítil-la	lítil-la	lítil-la
D. bún-um	bún-um	bún-um	litl-um	litl-um	litl-um
A. bún-a	bún-ar	búin.	litl-a	litl-ar	lítil.

DEFINITE.

	Sing.			Sing.	
N. bún-i	bún-a	bún-a	litl-i	litl-a	litl-a
G. bún-a	bún-u	bún-a	litl-a	litl-u	litl-a
D. bún-a	bún-u	bún-a	litl-a	litl-u	litl-a
A. bún-a	bún-u	bún-a	litl-a	litl-u	litl-a
	Plur.			Plur.	
bún-u.			litl-u.		

Indefinite.

	Sing.			Sing.		
	Masc.	Fem.	Neut.	Masc.	Fem.	Neut.
N.	laus-s	laus	laus-t	sæl-l	sæl	sæl-t
G.	laus-s	laus-ar	laus-s	sæl-s	sæl-lar	sæl-s
D.	laus-um	laus-i	laus-u	sæl-um	sæl-li	sæl-u
A.	laus-an	laus-a	laus-t	sæl-an	sæl-a	sæl-t.
	Plur.			Plur.		
N.	laus-ir	laus-a	laus	sæl-ir	sæl-ar	sæl
G.	laus-a	laus-a	laus-a	sæl-la	sæl-la	sæl-la
D.	laus-um	laus-um	laus-um	sæl-um	sæl-um	sæl-um
A.	laus-a	laus-ar	laus	sæl-a	sæl-um	sæl.

Definite.

	Sing.			Sing.		
N.	laus-i	laus-a	laus-a	sæl-i	sæl-a	sæl-a
G.	laus-a	laus-u	laus-a	sæl-a	sæl-u	sæl-a
D.	laus-a	laus-u	laus-a	sæl-a	sæl-u	sæl-a
A.	laus-a	laus-u	laus-a	sæl-a	sæl-u	sæl-a
	Plur.			Plur.		
	laus-u.			sæl-u.		

Like ***búinn*** are declined:

haldinn *holden* | heiðinn *heathen* | heppinn *lucky* | tekinn *taken*, which are contracted, since the termination begins with a vowel as, heiðnum. Those which have *a* in the first syllable admit a vowel-change when the *i* of the second syllable is rejected by contraction, and the ending begins with *u*, as hǒldnum.

Like ***sæll*** are declined:

brúnn *brown.*	fúll *foul.*	heill *whole.*	vænn *fair;*
brýnn *plain.*	háll *smooth.*	hreinn *pure.*	

and all others whose characteristic letter is *l* or *n*, with a diphthongic vowel.

When the root ends with an accented vowel, *t* is doubled in the neuter, as well as *r* in the genitive and dative feminine, and in the genitive plural.

Paradigms: blár *blue*, trúr *true, faithful.*

Indefinite.

	Sing.			Sing.		
	Masc.	Fem.	Neut.	Masc.	Fem.	Neut.
N.	blá-r	blá	blá-tt	trú-r	trú	trú-tt
G.	blá-s	blá-rrar	blá-s	trú-s	trú-rrar	trú-s
D.	blá-um	blá-rri	blá-u	trú-um	trú-rri	trú-a
A.	blá-an	blá-a	blá-tt	trú-an	trú-a	trú-tt

	PLUR.			PLUR.	
N. blá-ir	blá-ar	blá	trú-ir	trú-ar	trú
G. blá-rra	blá-rra	blá-rra	trú-rra	trú-rra	trú-rra
D. blá-um	blá-um	blá-um	trú-um	trú-um	trú-um
A. blá-a	blá-ar	blá	trú-a	trú	trú.

DEFINITE.

	SING.			SING.	
N. blá-i	blá-a	blá-a	trú-i	trú-a	trú-a
G. blá-a	blá-u	blá-a	trú-a	trú-u	trú-a
D. blá-a	blá-u	blá-a	trú-a	trú-u	trú-a
A. blá-a	blá-u	blá-a	trú-a	trú-u	trú-a.
	PLUR.			PLUR.	
blá-u.			trú-u.		

Thus are declined

frár *swift-footed.*	grár *grey.*	hlýr *lukewarm.*	nýr *new.*
frjór *fruitful.*	hár *high.*	mjór *small.*	þrár *enduring.*

Some adjectives which have a distinguishing radical consonant insert *j* or *v*, as in the inflection of nouns similarly characterized.

Paradigms: miðr *middle,* þykkr *thick.*

INDEFINITE.

	SING.			SING.	
Masc.	Fem.	Neut.	Masc.	Fem.	Neut.
N. mið-r	mið	mit-t	þykk-r	þykk	þyk-t
G. mið-s	mið-rar	mið-s	þykk-s	þykk-var	þykk-s
D. mið-jum	mið-ri	mið-ju	þykk-um	þykk-ri	þykk-u
A. mið-jan	mið-ja	mit-t	þykk-van	þykk-va	þyk-t
	PLUR.			PLUR.	
N. mið-ir	mið-jar	mið	þykk-vir	þykk-var	þykk
G. mið-ra	mið-ra	mið-ra	þykk-ra	þykk-ra	þykk-ra
D. mið-jum	mið-jum	mið-jum	þykk-um	þykk-um	þykk-um
A. mið-ja	mið-jar	mið	þykk-va	þykk-var	þykk

DEFINITE.

	SING.			SING.	
N. mið-i	mið-ja	mið-ja	þykk-vi	þykk-va	þykk-va
G. mið-ja	mið-ju	mið-ja	þykk-va	þykk-u	þykk-va
D. mið-ja	mið-ju	mið-ja	þykk-va	þykk-u	þykk-va
A. mið-ja	mið-ju	mið-ja	þykk-va	þykk-u	þykk-va
	PLUR.			PLUR.	
mið-ju.			þykku.		

Like *þykkr* are declined all adjectives with the root-vowel ö as, dökkr *gloomy*, glöggr *evident,* fölr *wan,* röskr *brisk;*

v before the dative termination *um*, *u* is frequently dropt as, þykkum, glöggum, yet we also find glöggvum, &c.

Some monosyllabic nouns, whose characteristic letter is *ó*, often insert *f* before the final letter as, mjór, mjófr, frjór, frjófr, sljór, sljófr *dull*. Hár can both admit and dispense with, the inserted *v*, and even reject the vowels of the inflections in *a* and *u* as, hávum, hám, háva, há.

In forms in *l, n, r,* where the masculine sign *r* is dropt, the vowel-rejection takes place in the same cases as in substantives of this form; thus, gamall, *dat.* gömlum, *acc.* gamlan, in the feminine gender gamla, *nom. plur. masc.* gamlir, and so on: likewise galinn, gölnum, galnir. A similar contraction often takes place in words in *-agr, -igr, -ugr*, for instance, heilagr helgr; heilagrar helgrar; heilögum, helgum *holy*. Likewise öfugr öfgr, öfugrar öfgrar *backward;* the abbreviated form, however, is generally used only where the inflection-ending begins with a vowel.

Paradigms: gamall *old;* galinn *silly*.

INDEFINITE.

	Sing.			Sing.	
Masc.	Fem.	Neut.	Masc.	Fem.	Neut.
N. gamal-l	gömul	gamal-t	galin-n	galin	galit
G. gamal-s	gamal-lar	gamal-s	galin-s	galin-nar	galin-s
D. göm-lum	gamal-li	göml-u	göld-um	galin-ni	göld-u
A. gaml-an	gam-la	gamal-t	galin-n	galin	galit
	Plur.			Plur.	
N. gaml-ir	gaml-ar	gömul	gald-ir	gald-ar	galin
G. gamal-la	gamal-la	gamal-la	galin-na	galin-na	galin-na
D. göml-um	göml-um	göml-um	göld-um	göld-um	göld-um
A. gaml-a	gaml-ar	gömul	gald-a	gald-ar	galin

DEFINITE.

	Sing.			Sing.	
N. gaml-i	gaml-a	gaml-a	gald-i	gald-a	gald-a
G. gaml-a	göml-u	gaml-a	gald-a	göld-u	gald-a
D. gaml-a	göml-u	gaml-a	gald-a	göld-u	gald-a
A. gaml-a	göml-u	gaml-a	gald-a	göld-u	gald-a
	Plur.			Plur.	
göml-u.			göld-u.		

Like *gamall* are declined svipall *fleeting,* þagall *silent.*

Like *galinn* are inflected

dulinn *hidden.*	skilinn *parted.*	vakinn *wakened.*	vaninn *wont.*
nakinn *naked.*	taminn *tamed.*	valinn *chosen.*	

Those words which form the neuter in *it,* also dissyllabic adjectives in *inn*, as well as *mikill* and lítill, have the accusative singular masculine in *inn*, as, for example, galinn, *acc.* galinn, not galnan, mikinn, litinn, not miklan, litlan (see above).

In all its abbreviated forms, *lítill* changes í to *i*, for instance, litlum, mikìll, under the same circumstances, often changes *i* to *y* as, myklan, myklum.

The endings *-rar, -ri,* and *-ra* drop their *r* after *r* with a preceding consonant, since double *r* after a consonant could not be pronounced: thus, fagr *fair:*

INDEFINITE.

	SING.			PLUR.	
Masc.	Fem.	Neut.	Masc.	Fem.	Neut.
N. fagr	fögr	fagr-t	*N.* fagr-ir	fagr-ar	fögr
G. fagr-s	fagr-ar	fagr-s	*G.* fagr-a	fagr-a	fagr-a
D. fögr-um	fagr-i	fögr-u	*D.* fögr-um	fögr-um	fögr-um
A. fagr-an	fagr-a	fagr-t	*A.* fagr-a	fagr-ar	fögr.

DEFINITE.

SING.

Masc.	Fem.	Neut.
N. fagr-i	fagr-a	fagr-a
G. fagr-a	fögr-u	fagr-a
D. fagr-a	fögr-u	fagr-a
A. fagr-a	fögr-u	fagr-a

PLUR.

fögr-u.

Thus are inflected:

bitr *bitter.*	digr *fat.*	magr *meagre.*	vitr *wise.*
dapr *sad.*	lipr *supple.*	vakr *lively.*	

Some compound adjectives which end in *a* or *i* are indeclinable as, gagn-drepa *soaked,* sammæðra *born of the same mother*, jafnaldra *of equal age*, draumstoli *one who does not dream,* heilvita-i *sharp-witted,* einmana-i *without retinue.*

---

2. Comparison of Adjectives.

The terminations of the comparative degree *-ri*, and of the superlative *-str* are combined with the root by the vowel *i* or *a*; the former effects a vowel-change, and is dropt; the latter is retained; thus *-ri*, *-str* occur with a vowel-change, and *-ari*, *-astr* without it.

Paradigms:

with *-ri*, *-str*, and vowel-change.			with *-ari*, *-astr* without vowel-change.		
fagr	fegri	fegrstr	spakr	spakari	spakastr
fair	*fairer*	*fairest*	*wise*	*wiser*	*wisest*
stor	stœrri	stœrstr	gjöfull	gjöflari	gjöflastr
great	*greater*	*greatest*	*liberal*	*more liberal*	*most liberal*
lágr	lægri	lægstr	heppinn	heppnari	heppnastr
low	*lower*	*lowest*	*lucky*	*more lucky*	*most lucky*
ungr	yngri	yngstr	konung-ligr	konung-ligari	konungli-gastr
young	*younger*	*youngest*	*royal*	*more royal*	*most royal*
þröngr	þrengri	þrengstr	kringlóttr	kringlót-tari	kringlót-tastr
narrow	*narrower*	*narrowest*			
djúpr	dýpri	dýpstr			
deep	*deeper*	*deepest*	*round*	*rounder*	*roundest.*

The word mjór *small*, does not undergo a vowel-change in the comparative and superlative which are *mjórri*, *mjóstr*.

Some adjectives are compared with either form, as:

deep djúpr, djúpari *and* dýpri, djúpastr *and* dýpstr
dear dýrr, dýrari *and* dýrri, dýrastr *and* dýrstr
new nýr, nýari *and* nýrri, nýastr *and* nýstr
black dökkr, dökkvari *and* dekkri, dökkvastr *and* dekkstr
fair fagr, fagrari *and* fegri, fagrastr *and* fegrstr
liberal gjöfull, gjöflari *and* gjöfulli, gjöflastr *and* gjöfulstr.

The latter form is the oldest and the best.

Some adjectives take *i* in the comparative and *a* in the superlative as, sæll *happy*, sælli, sælastr; hreinn *pure*, hreinni, hreinastr.

Diphthongal vowel roots double the *r* of the comparative, as: hár *high*, hærri, hæstr; nýr *new*, nýrri, nýstr; fár *few*, færri, fæstr.

The inflection of comparatives, however formed, is invariable, whether they are used definitely or indefinitely, as:

	Sing.		
	Masc.	Fem.	Neut.
N.	hvatari	hvatari	hvatara
G.	hvatara	hvatari	hvatara
D.	»	»	»
A.	»	»	»

Plur.

hvatari.

Sometimes the *dat. plur.* ends in -*um* as, fleirum, stærrum.

All participles present active in -*andi*, when used as adjectives, are declined like the comparatives; occasionally the *dat. plur.* ends in -*um* with or without the vowel-change, as: lifandum mönnum *to living men.*

The superlative however formed, is declined in the same manner as the positive; thus,

	Indefinite.			Definite.		
	Sing.			Sing.		
	Masc.	Fem.	Neut.	Masc.	Fem.	Neut.
N.	hvatastr	hvötust	hvatast	hvatasti	hvatasta	hvatasta
G.	hvatasts	hvatastrar	hvatasts	hvatasta	hvötustu	hvatasta
D.	hvötustum	hvatastri	hvötustu	»	»	»
A.	hvatastan	hvatasta	hvatast	»	»	»
	Plur.			Plur.		
N.	hvatastir	hvatastar	hvötust	hvötustu.		
G.	hvatastra	hvatastra	hvatastra			
D.	hvötustum	hvötustum	hvötustum			
A.	hvatasta	hvatastar	hvötust.			

Of those words which express a relative position or situation there can be no adjectival positives, but only comparatives and superlatives, the root being a substantive, preposition, or adverb, as:

		Comp.	Sup.
northwards	norðr	nyrðri nörðri norðri	nyrðstr nörðstr norðastr
eastwards	austr	eystri	austastr
southwards	suðr	syðri suðri	syðstr synstr
westwards	vestr	vestri	vestastr
forwards	fram	frémri	fremstr
behind	aptr	eptri aptari	epstr aptastr
nether	niðr	niðri neðri	niðstr neðstr
out	út	ýtri	ýstr

		Comp.	Sup.
in	inn	innri	innstr, instr
over	of / yfir	efri / öfri	efstr / öfstr / ofarstr
soon	áðr	æðri	æðstr
late	síð	síðari	síðastr
before	for	fyrri	fyrstr
rather	heldr	heldri	helzt
near	ná	nærri	næstr
up	upp		ypparstr
far	fjarri / fjærri	firri	firstr / fjærstr
seldom	sjaldan	sjaldnari	sjaldnastr
behind		hindri	hindstr.

Adjectives, which have no comparative on account of their ending, but the meaning of which admits of degrees of comparison, express them augmentatively or diminutively by means of the adverbs,

meir *more*,	mest *most*,	*or* heldr, helzt;
minnr *less*,	minnst *least*,	*or* síðr, sízt.

The preterite participle in *-inn*, used as an adjective, is inflected like búinn; those terminating in *-dr*, *-ðr*, *-tr*, like hvatr, as follows:

Singular.

	Masc.	Fem.	Neut.	Masc.	Fem.	Neut.
N.	vakin-n	vakin	vaki-t	vakið-r	vakið	vaki-t
G.	vakin-s	vakin-nar	vakin-s	vakið-s	vakið-rar	vakið-s
D.	vökn-um	vakin-ni	vökn-u	vökt-um	vakið-ri	vökt-u
A.	vakin-n	vakn-a	vaki-t	vakt-an	vakt-a	vaki-t

Singular.
(Continuation.)

	Masc.	Fem.	Neut.
N.	vakt-r	vökt	vakt
G.	vakt-s	vakt-ar	vakt-s
D.	vökt-um	vakt-ri	vökt-u
A.	vakt-an	vakt-a	vakt

Plural.

	Masc.	Fem.	Neut.	Masc.	Fem.	Neut.
N.	vakn-ir	vakn-ar	vakin	vakt-ir	vakt-ar	vakið
G.	vakin-na	vakin-na	vakin-na	vakið-ra	vakið-ra	vakið-ra
D.	vökn-um	vökn-um	vökn-um	vökt-um	vökt-um	vökt-um
A.	vakn-a	vakn-ar	vakin	vakt-a	vakt-ar	vakið

Plural.
(Continuation.)

	Masc.	Fem.	Neut.
N.	vakt-ir	vakt-ar	vökt
G.	vakt-ra	vakt-ra	vakt-ra
D.	vökt-um	vökt-um	vökt-um
A.	vakt-a	vakt-ar	vökt.

Participial adjectives in *-aðr* are declined regularly, but do not drop the *a*.

ANOMALOUS ADJECTIVES.

Some adjectives form their comparative and superlative irregularly, or from an obsolete positive, as:

góðr *good*	betri *better* skárri*	beztr *best* skástr*
illr *bad* vándr	verri *worse*	verstr *worst*
mikill *much* (*great*)	meiri *more*	mestr *most*
lítill *little*	minni *less*	minnstr *least.*
margr *much*	fleiri *more*	flestr *most*
gamall *old*	eldri *older* ellri *elder*	elstr *oldest*, *eldest.*

* diminutive forms.

CHAPTER IV.

OF PRONOUNS.

These are divided into six classes, viz; personal, possessive, demonstrative, interrogative, relative, and indefinite pronouns.

1. Personal Pronouns.

Without distinction of gender:

Singular.

	1st pers.	2nd pers.	3rd pers.
N.	ek *or* eg *I*	þú *thou*	—
G.	mín *of me*	þín *of thee*	sín *of one's self*
D.	mèr *to me*	þèr *to thee*	sèr *to one's self*
A.	mik *me*	þik *thee*	sik, sig *one's self.*

Dual.

N.	við *or* vit *we two*	þið *or* þit *ye two*	—
G.	okkar *of us two*	ykkar *of you two*	—
D.	okkr *to us two*	ykkr *to you two*	—
A.	okkr *us two*	ykkr *you two*	—

Plural.

N. vèr *we*	þèr, èr *ye* or *you*	—
G. vár *of us*	yðar, yðvar *of you*	sín *of themselves*
D. oss *to us*	yðr *to you*	sèr *to themselves*
A. oss *us*	yðr *you*	sik *themselves.*

With distinction of gender:

Masc.	Fem.
N. hann *he*	hún, hon *she*
G. hans *of him*	hennar *of her*
D. hánum, honum *to him*	henni *to her*
A. hann *him*	hana *her.*

The plural, as well as the neuter, is supplied by the demonstrative pronoun sá, sú, þat.

Ek is frequently combined in one form with the word immediately preceding as, fæk, emk, ætlak, which are the 1st pers. sing. pres. ind. of the verbs fá *to get,* vera *to be,* and ætla *to think.*

Þú in composition becomes *tú* or *dú* according to the character of the foregoing letter as, skaltú *shalt thou,* mundú *must thou.* Should *tt* occur after a consonant only one *t* is written as, veitstú *for* veitst þú *knowest thou.* When it is compounded with imperatives the accent is dropt as, sjáðu *see thou,* gakktu *do thou go.*

---

2. Possessive Pronouns.

These are formed from the genitive of the personal pronoun; they are as follows:

minn	mín	mitt *mine*	ykkarr	ykkur	ykkart *your* (*of two*).
þinn	þín	þitt *thine*	várr	vár	várt *our* (*of many*).
sinn	sín	sitt *his, hers, its*	yðarr	yður	yðart *your* (*do.*) or,
okkarr	okkur	okkart *our* (*of two*)	yðvarr	yður	yðvart.

They are inflected thus:

Singular.

	Masc.	Fem.	Neut.	Masc.	Fem.	Neut.
N.	minn	mín	mitt	okkarr	okkur	okkart
G.	míns	minnar	míns	okkars	okkarrar	okkars
D.	mínum	minni	mínu	okkrum	okkarri	okkru
A.	minn	mína	mitt	okkaru	okkra	okkart

Plural.

N.	mínir	mínar	mín	okkrir	okkrar	okkur
G.	minna	minna	minna	okkarra	okkarra	okkarra
D.	mínum	mínum	mínum	okkrum	okkrum	okkrum
A.	mína	mínar	mín	okkra	okkrar	okkur.

As *minn* are inflected þinn and sinn, and as *okkarr* are declined ykkarr and yðarr.

Várr is thus inflected:

	Singular.		
	Masc.	Fem.	Neut.
N.	várr	vár	várt
G.	várs	várrar	várs
D.	várum	várri	váru
A.	váru	vára	várt
	Plural.		
N.	várir	várar	vár
G.	várra	várra	várra
D.	várum	várum	várum
A.	vára	várar	vár.

No possessive is formed from *hann*, *hún*; but the genitives *hans*, *hennar*, and in the plural *þeirra* (from *þat*) only are used.

The dative of the personal pronoun is sometimes used in a possessive sense as, með hnefa mèr *with my fist*, þèr til bana *to thy death*, á hendi sèr *in his hand*.

---

3. Demonstrative Pronouns.

These are three in number, *viz.* sá, sú, þat *he, she, it, that*; þessi, þessi, þetta, *this*; hinn, hin, hitt *that*; the last is also used as the definite article.

	Sing.			Plur.		
	Masc.	Fem.	Neut.	Masc.	Fem.	Neut.
N.	sá	sú	þat	þeir	þær	þau
G.	þess	þeirrar	þess	þeirra	þeirra	þeirra
D.	þeim	þeirri	því	þeim	þeim	þeim
A.	þann	þá	þat	þá	þær	þau.

Instead of *þeim* the older form *þeima* is often met with.

Sá, sú, þat is likewise used as a definite article. For *sá* and *sú* the old form *sjá* is often employed.

	Sing.			Plur.		
	Masc.	Fem.	Neut.	Masc.	Fem.	Neut.
N.	þessi	þessi	þetta	þessir	þessar	þessi
G.	þessa	þessarrar	þessa	þessarra	þessarra	þessarra
D.	þessum	þessarri	þessu	þessum	þessum	þessum
A.	þenna	þessa	þetta	þessa	þessar	þessi.

This pronoun was originally formed from *sá*, whose ancient form *þerr* in the nominative appears here again with *si* added; thus several obsolete forms are to be found, which show that it was at one time customary only to decline *þerr* and add *si* without inflection, thus; þersi *for* þessi; þeimsi *for* þessum, þvísa *for* þessu, þannsi *for* þenna.

For the inflections of hinn see the article, p. 11.

Besides these, hann, hún, is sometimes used as an article with proper names as, hann Sigurðr, hún þurídr.

Samr, söm, samt *the same,* is declined like a regular adjective; but *hinn* is often prefixed as, hin sama *fem.*, hit sama *neuter*.

The following, slíkr, slík, slíkt; þvílíkr, þvílík, þvílíkt; þessligr, þesslig, þessligt, all signifying *such,* are regularly inflected.

---

4. Interrogative Pronouns.

These are, hvar, hvárr *who* (*of two*)? hverr *who* (*of many*)? and hvílíkr *what kind of?*

The pronoun *hvar* is defective; not only does it want the feminine and the plural, but the nominative and accusative masculine singular; both forms are supplied by hverr *who* (*of many*)?

	Sing.		
	Masc.	Fem.	Neut.
N.	(hvar)	—	hvat
G.	hvess	—	hvess
D.	hveim	—	hví
A.	(hvann)	—	hvat.

In usual discourse, *hvat* is only used as a pronoun, and *hví* as an adjective.

Hvárr *who* (*of two*)? takes *hvorn* for *hvoran* in the sing. acc. masc.

	Sing.			Plur.		
	Masc.	Fem.	Neut.	Masc.	Fem.	Neut.
N.	hvár-r	hvár	hvár-t	hvár-ir	hvár-ar	hvár
G.	hvár-s	hvár-rar	hvár-s	hvár-ra	hvár-ra	hvár-ra
D.	hvár-um	hvár-ri	hvár-u	hvár-um	hvár-um	hvár-um
A.	hvár-n	hvár-a	hvár-t	hvár-a	hvár-ar	hvár.

Hverr *who (of many)*? has *hvern* for *hverjan* in the sing. acc. masc., in the modern tongue.

	Sing.			Plur.		
	Masc.	Fem.	Neut.	Masc.	Fem.	Neut.
N.	hver-r	hver	hver-t	hver-ir	hverj-ar	hver
G.	hver-s	hver-rar	hver-s	hver-ra	hver-ra	hver-ra
D.	hverj-um	hver-ri	hverj-u	hverj-um	hverj-um	hverj-um
A.	hverj-an	hverj-a	hver-t	hverj-a	hverj-ar	hver.

The idea, "what kind of?" is expressed by a compound of the neuter hví *what* and líkr *like*, thus:

	Sing.			Plur.		
	Masc.	Fem.	Neut.	Masc.	Fem.	Neut.
N.	hvílík-r	hvílík	hvílík-t	hvílík-ir	hvílík-ar	hvílík
G.	hvílík-s	hvílík-rar	hvílík-s	hvílík-ra	hvílík-ra	hvílík-ra
D.	hvílík-um	hvílík-ri	hvílík-u	hvílík-um	hvílík-um	hvílík-um
A.	hvílík-an	hvílík-a	hvílík-t	hvílík-a	hvílík-ar	hvílík.

---

5. Relative Pronouns.

Properly speaking, there are no relative pronouns, but the interrogatives *hverr* and *hvílíkr* are used in their stead, as well as the demonstrative *sá, sú, þat,* either alone, or more usually in connection with the particle *er* or *sem* as, sá er *he who,* þat sem *that which. Er* and *sem* likewise answer to the German "so" *who, which, that.*

---

6. Indefinite Pronouns.

Hvártveggi *either of two, both,* has a double inflection, and is thus declined:

	Singular.		
	Masc.	Fem.	Neut.
N.	hvár-tveggi	hvár-tveggi	hvár-tveggja
G.	hvárs-tveggja	hvárrar-tveggju	
D.	hvárum-tveggja	hvárri-tveggju / hváru-tveggju	hváru-tveggja
A.	hvárn-tveggja	hvára-tveggju	hvár-tveggja
	Plural.		
N.	hvárir-tveggja		
G.	hvárra-tveggja / hvárra-tveggju		
D.	hvárum-tveggja / hvárum-tveggjum		
A.	hvára-tveggju	hvár-tveggju	hvár-tveggi.

In the same way is inflected annartveggi *one of two.*

Annarr-hvárr *each other, every other,* is doubly declined as, *fem.* önnur-hvár, *neut.* annat-hvárt. Hvárr-annan *one another* (*of two*) and hverr-annan *one another* (*of many*) are likewise inflected independently of each other.

Einn-hver, einhver, eitthvert *every one, each.*

Hverr-einn, hverteitt, hvateitt *every, each.*

Sum-hverr *somebody, anybody, some one, any one.*

Sinn-hvárr, sinhvár, sitthvárt, sitthvat *each his own, each one's.* More usual is sinnhverr, sinhver, sitthvert as: þeir líta sinn í hverja átt *each looks to his own side.*

Sèrhverr, sèrhver, sèrhvert, sèrhvat *each.*

Nökkurr *some one, any,* whose various forms in the nominative are nakkvarr, nekkvarr, nekkverr, nekkurr, nokkvarr, nokkvorr, nokkverr, nökkverr and nokkurr, is thus declined:

	Sing.			Plur.		
	Masc.	Fem.	Neut.	Masc.	Fem.	Neut.
N.	nökkur-r	nökkur	nökkut	nökkur-ir	nökkur-ar	nökkur
G.	nökkur-s	nökkur-rar	nökkur-s	nökkur-ra	(*throughout*)	
D.	nökkur-um	nökkur-ri	nökkur-u	nökkur-um	(*throughout*)	
A.	nökkur-u	nökkur	nökkut	nökkur-a	nökkur-ar	nökkur.

Hvárigr, hvárig, hvárigt, *or* hvárugr, hvárug, hvárugt, means *neither* (*of the two*), and is used in connection with annarr as, hvárigr trúði öðrum *neither believed the other.*

From the neuter hvat, *dat.* hví, and *gen. plur.* vitna from viti *occasion, time* (French *fois*), is formed hvatvitna, *dat.* hvívitna *whatsoever.*

Hverrsem *or* hverrsem helzt *whoso* or *whosoever.*

Annarr *other, another, the one, the second,* is very irregular, and is thus declined:

	Sing.			Plur.		
	Masc.	Fem.	Neut.	Masc.	Fem.	Neut.
N.	annarr	önnur	annat	aðrir	aðrar	önnur
G.	annars	annarrar	annars	annarra	(*throughout*)	
D.	öðrum	annarri	öðru	öðrum	(*do.*)	
A.	annan	aðra	annat	aðra	aðrar	önnur.

Engi *none, no one,* is a compound of einn, ein, eitt and the negative particle *-gi, -ki,* and is thus declined:

	SING.			PLUR.		
	Masc.	Fem.	Neut.	Masc.	Fem.	Neut.
N.	engi	engi	ekki	engir	engar	engi
G.	enskis	engrar	enskis	engra	(*throughout.*)	
D.	engum	engri	engu	engum	(*do.*)	
A.	engan	enga	ekki	enga	engar	engi.

The indefinite person *one* (French *on*, Germ. *man*) is expressed either by the 3rd pers. sing. of the verb without a pronoun as, ok heyrði þat *and one heard that, and it was heard,* or by the plural menn *men* as, er menn tóku at drekka *when men took to drinking*; or lastly, by the modern form of maðr *man*.

The impersonal *there, it,* is expressed by *þat*, even though followed by a plural verb as, þat eru margir sem *there are many who*; still there is the regular form þeir eru margir *they are many*.

If many persons are implied, but only one is mentioned, the pronoun (mostly *sá*) usually stands in the plural, whilst the name connected with it remains in the singular number as, þeir Loki, *i. e., Loki and his mate*; þeir Gunnarr *Gunnarr and Sigurðr*; þeir Beli *Beli and Frey*; við þá Gunnar *towards Gunnarr and his folk*; vit Sigurðr *I and Sigurðr*. When words of different genders come together the pronoun is placed in the neut. plur., as, þau ýmis *now he, then she*; áttu þau *owned they* (*Jonak and Gudrun*); bæði þau *both they* (Randver and Svanhild).

CHAPTER V.

THE NUMERALS AND THEIR INFLECTIONS.

These are divided into cardinal and ordinal.

1. Cardinal Numbers.

1	einn, ein, eitt	10	tíu
2	tveir. tvær, tvö	11	ellifu
3	þrír, þrjár, þrjú	12	tólf
4	fjórir, fjórar, fjögur	13	þrettán
5	fimm	14	fjórtán
6	sex	15	fimtán
7	sjau (sjö)	16	sextán
8	átta	17	sjautján
9	níu	18	áttján

19	nitján	80	áttatíu
20	tuttugu	90	níutíu
21	tuttugu ok einn	100	hundrað, tíutíu
30	þrjátíu	110	hundrað ok tíu, ellifutíu
40	fjörutíu	120	hundrað ok tuttugu, stórt hundrað
50	fimtíu	200	tvö hundrað
60	sextíu	1000	þúsund.
70	sjautíu (sjötíu)		

An indeclinable form in *-tigi* is used adjectively, as: *dat.* þrjátigi mönnum *to thirty men.*

In modern Icelandic *-tíu* takes the place of *-tigir* or *-tigi*.

For declension of *einn*, see p. 11.

Tveir, þrír, and fjórir are thus declined:

	Masc.	Fem.	Neut.	Masc.	Fem.	Neut.	Masc.	Fem.	Neut.
N.	tveir	tvær	tvö	þrír	þrjár	þrjú	fjórir	fjórar	fjögur
G.	tveggja	(*throughout*)		þriggja	(*throughout*)		fjögurra	(*throughout*)	
D.	tveim	(*do.*)		þrim	(*do.*)		fjórum	(*do.*)	
A.	tvá	tvær	tvö	þrjá	þrjár	þrjú	fjóra	fjórar	fjögur.

The remainder, as far as tuttugu included, are indeclinable; but the succeeding, up to hundrað, are formed from the numeral substantive *tigr* (from tí *ten*), which is inflected like *siðr* in the 2nd declension, and governs the noun following it in the genitive, as:

fjórir	tigir	manna		*forty men*
fjögurra	tiga	—	*of*	—
fjórum	tigum	—	*to*	—
fjóra	tigu	—		—

Hundrað is a regularly inflected neuter:

Sing. nom.	hundrað	*Plur. nom.*	hundruð
gen.	——s	*gen.*	hundraða
dat.	——i	*dat.*	hundruðum
acc.	——	*acc.*	——

þúsund is feminine, and is thus declined:

Sing. nom.	þúsund	*Plur. nom.*	þúsundir
gen.	þúsundar	*gen.*	þúsunda
dat.	——(u)	*dat.*	——um
acc.	——	*acc.*	——ir.

The neuter þúshundrað, *plur.* þúshundruð, is also used, meaning a thousand, properly, 1200.

As the ancient Icelanders used the duodecimal as well as the decimal mode of numeration, they signified by the *great hundred* (stórt hundrað) 120, as opposed to the *small hundred* (100) which was sometimes expressed by tíutigir; so that *hálft hundrað* formerly counted for 60.

Báðir *both*, which resembles *tveir*, and is a numeral adjective, is thus declined:

	Masc.	Fem.	Neut.
N.	báðir	báðar	bæði
G.	beggja	(*throughout*)	
D.	báðum	(*do.*)	
A.	báða	báðar	bæði.

The date of the year would be thus expressed: þúsund átta hundrað sextíu níu 1869.

---

2. Ordinal Numbers.

The first	fyrsti, fyrsta, fyrsta	*The*	17*th*	sjautjándi
— *second*	annarr, önnur, annat	—	18*th*	áttjándi
— *third*	þriðji, þriðja, þriðja	—	19*th*	nítjándi
— *fourth*	fjórði, fjórða, fjórða	—	20*th*	tuttugast
— 5*th*	fimti	—	30*th*	þrítugasti
— 6*th*	sètti	—	40*th*	fertugasti
— 7*th*	sjaundi	—	50*th*	fimtugasti
— 8*th*	átti (áttundi)	—	60*th*	sextugasti
— 9*th*	níundi	—	70*th*	sjautugasti
— 10*th*	tíundi	—	80*th*	áttatugasti
— 11*th*	ellifti	—	90*th*	nítugasti
— 12*th*	tólfti	—	100*th*	hundraðasti
— 13*th*	þrettándi	—	110*th*	— ok tíundi
— 14*th*	fjórtándi	—	120*th*	— ok tuttugasti
— 15*th*	fimtándi	—	200*th*	tvö hundraðasti
— 16*th*	sextándi	—	1000*th*	þúsundasti.

J is inserted before *a* and *u* of the different inflections of þriði.

The collective numbers, or numeral substantives, are:

fimt	*five*	*in number*
sjaund	*seven* —	—
tigr	*ten* —	—
tylft	*twelve* —	—

Fimt and sjaund are used solely for a space of five or seven days; both are feminine words as well as tylft.

There are several temporals as, from nótt *night*, come einnætt *one night old*, nætrgamalt *night old*, and from vetr *winter*, *year* vetrgamalt *winter old*, *year old*, tvævett *two winters old*.

To signify a period of three or four days the compounds *þrínættingr* and *fjórnættingr* are used. To designate 30,

40, &c. days, the neuter of the numerals included in *-ugr* is used substantively, as: þrítugt, fertugt, &c.

The distributive numerals are:

tvennr	*two at a time*
þrennr	*three — — —*
fern	*four — — —*:

they correspond with the Latin termination *-arius*, and are regular.

Numeral adjectives, in tens from 20 to 70 inclusive, are formed by *-tugr*; from 80 to 120 inclusive, by *-ræðr*; and they are used both of age, measure, and the like. Thus,

tvítugr	*containing*	20	áttræðr	*containing*	80
þrítugr	—	30	níræðr	—	90
fertugr	—	40	tíræðr	—	100
fimtugr	—	50	ellifuræðr	—	110
sextugr	—	60	tólfræðr	—	120.
sjautugr	—	70			

By placing *hálf* before such a numeral a number of magnitude can be signified which is five less, *e. g.* hálffertugr, comprising three tens and a half, *i. e.*, 35; yet this mode of designation is chiefly applied to ships which reckon by their number of oars, and to the age of persons as, hálf þrítugt skip *a 25 oared ship*, hálf þrítugr maðr *a man 25 years old*.

Multiplicative numerals are formed by adding *faldr* (*fem.* föld, *neut.* falt) to cardinal numbers. They are used and declined like adjectives, as: einfaldr *simple*, tvífaldr *twofold*. From these are formed verbs in *-falda*, as: tvaufalda *to double*, þrefalda *to treble*, margfalda *to multiply*.

Fractional numbers, with 1 as a numerator, are formed by *-ungr*, which is added to the neuter of the ordinal after *a* is dropt, as: þriðjungr $\frac{1}{3}$, fjórðungr $\frac{1}{4}$. Numeral Adverbs: tvisvar *twice*, þrisvar *thrice*. The others are expressed by the dative of sinn *time*, as: einu sinni *once*, fjórum sinnum *four times*. Tveim sinnum, þrim sinnum, *or* tvisvar sinnum, þrisvar sinnum are also used; but the last are tautological. The article *hit* is prefixed to fyrsta, annat, þriðja sinn (*the first, second, third time*), but not necessarily so. "This time" is expressed by þetta sinn. Instead of *sinn*, the neuters skeið (*lapse of time*) and skipti (*division*) are also used, as: hit fyrsta skipti, annat skeið, and so on. Sometimes in place of the article the preposition í *in* is employed, as: í fjórða sinn *for the fourth time*.

CHAPTER VI.

VERBS.

Icelandic verbs are active, passive, or neuter.

A verb active expresses an action, and necessarily implies an agent, and an object acted upon as; at elska *to love;* ek elska GuÐ *I love God.*

A verb passive, which is formed by the addition of *st* or *z* to the active, expresses the receiving of an action, and necessarily implies an object acted upon, and an agent by which it is acted upon as; at elskast *to be loved;* GuÐ elskast af hánum *God is loved by him.*

The passive is likewise expressed by the auxiliary verbs *verða* and *vera* with the past participle of the principal verb as;

ek verð	borinn	*I am born*
— varð	—	*I was —*
— em	—	*I have been born*
— var	—	*I had — —*

still *em* is also used for the present, *var* for the preterite tense: *Ex. var* hann harðliga freistad *he was sorely tempted; var* skipt liðinu í tvá staði · *the army was divided into two sections.*

A verb neuter expresses neither action nor passion, but being, or a state of being, as; ek em *I am,* ek sef *I sleep*, ek sit. *I sit.*

When a verb expresses an action in which the agent acts, and is acted upon by himself, it is said to be in the reflective form as; at skammast sín *to be ashamed of one's self.*

The termination *sk,* which is now also written *st* or *z,* was originally simply a contraction of the reflective pronoun *sik,* corresponding to our *self*, or more exactly, to the French reflective *se,* so that *at kallast* was equivalent to *to call one's self*, or the French *s'appeler.* It gradually assumed a passive force, and there are a few instances of its employment as such by classic writers in the best ages of Old-Norse literature.

Those verbs which have a passive form with an active meaning as, at öðlast *to obtain*, are called *deponent* verbs; they are only few in number.

When an action is conceived without a definite subject from which it proceeds, the verb is called *impersonal*, and is used only in the third personal singular, the place of the subject being supplied by the neuter personal pronoun þat *it* as; þat snjóar *it snows*.

All verbs are arranged in two classes answering to the *strong* and *weak* forms of the German grammarians. The former consists in a change of the radical vowel in the preterite tense and past participle; the latter admits of the addition of vocal elements to the root, for example:

	Infinitive.	Preterite.	Past part.
Strong. —	syngja	sőng	sunginn
	to sing	*sang*	*sung*
	stela	stal	stolinn (English *en*)
	to steal	*stole*	*stolen*
Weak. —	kalla	kallaða (Eng. *ed*; German *te* or *ete*).	kallaðr
	to call	*called*	*called.*

The principle on which this nomenclature is founded is, that the power of varying a word by change of its more unessential constituents, without external aid in the way of composition or addition of syllables, implies a certain vitality, a certain innate, organic strength not possessed by roots capable of variation only by the incorporation or addition of foreign elements. The weak inflection is the *regular*, the strong, *the irregular*, form of the older grammarians, and the latter is the more ancient of the two modes of inflection; therefore the more appropriate appellations would be the *old* and *new* modes.

A small number of verbs have an anomalous, or, more properly speaking, a mixed conjugation. that is, a mode of conjugation consisting of a combination of the strong and weak.

The first class has seven conjugations whose preterite indicative is always monosyllabic, having a consonantal ending with change of vowel; the past participle is inflected in *inn, in, it.*

The second class has two conjugations whose preterite indicative is always unchanged; the past participle ends in *dr, d, t.*

There are therefore nine conjugations in which every regular and irregular verb is included.

There are four moods in each conjugation, the indicative, conjunctive, imperative, and infinitive; but only two tenses, the present and preterite, can be expressed by inflection.

The other tenses are formed by means of auxiliary verbs.

In the first three of the moods above-named there are the two numbers, singular and plural, and the usual persons, the personal pronoun being placed before the verb, since the difference of persons, especially in the passive voice, is frequently undefined. The participles are, the present active and the past. The infinitive always contains the root-vowel. The present and preterite tense, as well as the past participle or supine, are the most important of the tenses.

The auxiliary verbs of tense are, hafa *to have*, vera *to be*, verða *to become;* and they are thus conjugated:

At hafa *to have.*

INDICATIVE MOOD.

Present Tense.

SING.		PLUR.	
ek hefi,	*I have,*	vèr höfum,	*we have,*
þú hefir,	*thou hast;*	þèr hafið,	*you have,*
hann hefir,	*he has;*	þeir hafa,	*they have.*

Preterite.

ek hafði,	*I had,*	vèr höfðum,	*we had,*
þú hafðir,	*thou hadst,*	þèr höfðuð,	*you had,*
hann hafði,	*he had;*	þeir höfðu,	*they had.*

CONJUNCTIVE MOOD.

Present Tense.

SING.		PLUR.	
ek hafi,	*I may have,*	vèr hafim,	*we may have,*
þú hafir,	*thou mayest have,*	þèr hafið,	*you may have,*
hann hafi,	*he may have;*	þeir hafi,	*they may have.*

Preterite.

ek hefði,	*I might have,*	vèr hefðim,	*we might have,*
þú hefðir,	*thou mightest have,*	þèr hefðið,	*you might have,*
hann hefði,	*he might have;*	þeir hefði,	*they might have.*

IMPERATIVE MOOD.	INFINITIVE MOOD.
SING. hafðu, *have thou;*	at hafa, *to have.*
PLUR. höfum, *let us have,*	*Pres. part.* hafandi, *having,*
hafið, *have ye.*	*Past part.* haft, *had.*

Hafa is often used with a past participle agreeing, like an adjective, in gender and case with the object, *e. g.*, er þeir höfðu feldan höfðingja liðsins *when they had struck down the chiefs of the people*. It is also used with the supine passive as; er þeir höfðu viðtalast *when they had spoken together*.

At vera *to be.*

INDICATIVE MOOD.

Present Tense.

SING.		PLUR.	
ek em,	*I am,*	vèr erum,	*we are,*
þú ert,	*thou art,*	þèr eruð,	*you are,*
hann er,	*he is;*	þeir eru,	*they are.*

Preterite.

ek var,	*I was,*	vèr várum,	*we were,*
þú vart,	*thou wast,*	þèr váruð,	*you were,*
hann var,	*he was;*	þeir váru,	*they were.*

CONJUNCTIVE MOOD.

Present Tense.

SING.		PLUR.	
ek sè,	*I may be,*	vèr sèim,	*we may be,*
þú sèr,	*thou mayest be,*	þèr sèið,	*you may be,*
hann sè,	*he may be;*	þeir sèi,	*they may be.*

Preterite.

ek væri,	*I might be,*	vèr værim,	*we might be,*
þú værir,	*thou mightest be,*	þèr værið,	*you might be,*
hann væri,	*he might be;*	þeir væri,	*they might be.*

IMPERATIVE MOOD.				INFINITIVE MOOD.
veri,	*let me be.*	verum,	*let us be,*	at vera, *to be.*
ver-tu,	*be thou,*	verit,	*be ye,*	*Pres. part.* verandi, *being.*
veri,	*let him be;*	veri,	*let them be.*	*Past part.* verit, *been.*

Vera, with *at* and the infinitive of other verbs, signifies a definite time, as: ek em at skrifa *I am just going to write.*

A thoroughly past time, which we denote by laying an emphasis on the auxiliary verb, is expressed periphrastically in Icelandic by the phrase *ek embúinn,* followed by the infinitive with *at,* as: ek em búinn at skrifa *I have* (already) *written.*

At verða *to become.*

INDICATIVE MOOD.		CONJUNCTIVE MOOD.	
Present.	Preterite.	Present.	Preterite.
I become.	*I became.*	*I may become.*	*I might become.*
S. ek verð,	S. ek varð,	S. ek yrði,	S. ek varð,
þú verðr,	þú varð,	þú yrðir,	þú varð,
hann verðr;	hann varð;	hann yrði,	hann varð;
P. vèr verðum,	P. vèr urðum,	P. vèr yrðim,	P. vèr urðum,
þèr verðið,	þèr urðuð,	þèr yrðið,	þèr urðuð,
þeir verða.	þeir urðu.	þeir yrði.	þeir urðu.

Imperative Mood.	Infinitive Mood.
verð-ðu *do thou become*	at verða *to become.*
Pres. part. verðandi *becoming.*	*Past part.* orðinn *become.*

FIRST CLASS.

Sign-Forms.

1. Infinitive. 2. 1 pers. sing. pres. ind. 3. 1 pers. sing. pret. ind. 4. 1 pers. plur. pret. ind. 5. Past part.

First Conjugation.

Vowel of the pret. *a*, plur. *u*.

Characteristics. — Everywhere a short vowel. The root-endings generally double, or liquids connected with mutes: rarely double mutes. Vowel of the infinitive *e* (seldom *ja*); *i* before *nn* (except *brenna, renna*), *nd* and *ng*; *y* before *ngv*, *ö* before *ggv, kkv*, yet the pres. of *slöggva* is *slyng*. Past part. has *o*; but *u* before *nn, nd, ng*. Strong *v*-vowel-changed words have *ö* for *a* in the pret. sing. ind.

In the preterite tense, as well as in the 2 pers. sing. of the imperative, where the root-termination likewise appears, *d* after *l* becomes *t*; after *n* both *d* and *g* are changed into their corresponding thin letters *t* and *k*, with assimilation of *n*.

At brenna *to burn.*

Active Voice.

Indicative Mood.		Conjunctive Mood.	
Present.	Preterite.	Present.	Preterite.
I burn.	*I burned.*	*I may burn.*	*I might burn.*
Sing.	Sing.	Sing.	Sing.
ek brenn,	ek brann,	ek brenni,	ek brynni,
þú brennr,	þú brannt,	þú brennir,	þú brynnir,
hann brennr;	hann brann;	hann brenni;	hann brynni;
Pl.	Pl.	Pl.	Pl.
vèr brennum,	vèr brunnum,	vèr brennim,	vèr brynnim,
þèr brennið,	þèr brunnuð,	þèr brennið,	þèr brynnið,
þeir brenna.	þeir brunnu.	þeir brenni.	þeir brynni.

Imperative Mood.	Infinitive Mood.
brenn-ðu, *do thou burn,*	at brenna *to burn.*
brennum, *let us burn,*	*Pres. part.* brennandi *burning,*
brennið, *do ye burn.*	*Past part.* brunninn *burned.*

To this conjugation belong the following verbs:

	inf.	pres.	pret. sing.	pret. plur.	past part.
to strike	bella	bell	ball	bullum	bollinn
- *help*	berga *or* bjarga	berg	barg	burgum	borginn
- *swing*	bregða	bregð	brá	brugðum	brugðinn
- *burst*	bresta	brest	brast	brustum	brostinn
- *fall*	detta	dett	datt	duttum	dottinn
- *drink*	drekka	drekk	drakk	drukkum	drukkinn
- *sound*	gella *or* gjalla	gell	gall	gullum	gollinn
- *pay*	gjalda	geld	galt	guldum	goldinn
- *crackle*	gnesta	gnest	gnast	gnustum	gnostinn
- *help*	hjálpa	help	halp	hulpum	hólpinn
- *tingle*	hvella	hvell	hvall	hullum	hollinn
- *turn round*	hverfa	hverf	hvarf	hurfum	horfinn
- *run*	renna	renn	rann	runnum	runninn
- *shake*	skjálfa	skelf	skalf	skulfum	skolfinn
- *ring*	skella	skell	skall	skullum	skollinn
- *let slip*	sleppa	slepp	slapp	sluppum	sloppinn
- *jingle*	smella	smell	small	smullum	smollinn
- *touch*	snerta	snert	snart	snurtum	snortinn
- *sprout*	spretta	sprett	spratt	spruttum	sprottinn
- *swill*	svelgja	svelg	svalg	sulgum	solginn
- *swell*	svella	svell	svall	sullum	sollinn
- *hunger*	svelta	svelt	svalt	sultum	soltinn
- *roll*	velta	velt	valt	ultum	oltinn
- *wipe off*	sverfa	sverf	svarf	surfum	sorfinn
- *boil*	vella	vell	vall	ullum	ollinn
- *become*	verða	verð	varð	urðum	orðinn
- *lay (eggs)*	verpa	verp	varp	urpum	orpinn
- *lessen*	þverra	þverr	þvarr	þurrum	þorrinn
- *bind*	binda	bind	batt	bundum	bundinn
- *find*	finna	finn	fann	funnum *or* fundum	funninn *or* fundinn
- *throw down*	hrinda	hrind	hratt	hrundum	hrundinn
- *spin*	spinna	spinn	spann	spunnum	spunninn
- *spur*	spirna *or* spurna	spirn	sparn	spurnum	sporninn
- *spring*	springa	spring	sprakk	sprungum	sprunginn
- *sting*	stinga	sting	stakk	stungum	stunginn
- *wind*	vinda	vind	vatt	undum	undinn
- *win*	vinna	vinn	vann	unnum	unninn
- *go forward*	hrökkva	hrökk	hrökk	hrukkum	hrukkinn
- *sink*	sökkva	sökk	sökk	sukkum	sokkinn
- *throw*	slöggva	slyng	slöng	slungum	slunginn
- *spring*	stökkva	stökk	stökk	stukkum	stukkinn
- *sing*	syngva / syngja	syng	söng	sungum	sunginn
- *press*	þryngva	þryng	þröng	þrungum	þrunginn.

SECOND CONJUGATION.

Vowel of the pret. *a*, plur. *á*.

Characteristics. — Simple root-vowel: vowel of the infinitive *e* (originally *i*). In some words a root-consonant accompanying *j* has preserved the original vowel *i*, and in others the original *ve*, *u* has passed over to *o*. The past part. has the vowel *e*, unless the root-consonant is a liquid, or the original vowel has been *ve*, for in such cases it becomes *o*. The pret. sing. in words with the root-consonant *g* should properly become *ag*; but here *g* falls away, and the vowel becomes lang *á*, as in vega, *pret.* vá, &c.

At gefa *to give.*

INDICATIVE MOOD.		CONJUNCTIVE MOOD.	
Present.	Preterite.	Present.	Preterite.
I give.	*I gave.*	*I may give.*	*I might give.*
S. ek gef,	S. ek gaf,	S. ek gefi,	S. ek gæfi,
þú gefr,	þú gaft,	þú gefir,	þú gæfir,
hann gefr;	hann gaf;	hann gefi;	hann gæfi;
P. vèr gefum,	P. vèr gáfum,	P. vèr gefim,	P. vèr gæfim,
þèr gefið,	þèr gáfuð,	þèr gefið,	þèr gæfið,
þeir gefa.	þeir gáfu.	þeir gefi.	þeir gæfi.

IMPERATIVE MOOD.	INFINITIVE MOOD.
gef-ðu, *do thou give,*	at gefa *to give.*
gefum, *let us give,*	*Pres. part.* gefandi, *giving.*
gefið, *do ye give.*	*Past part.* gefinn, *given.*

To this conjugation belong the following verbs:

	inf.	pres.	pret. sing.	pret. plur.	past part.
to slay	drepa	drep	drap	drápum	drepinn
- *eat*	eta	et	át	átum	etinn
- *inquire*	fregna	fregn	frá	frágum	freginn
- *get*	geta	get	gat	gátum	getinn
- *say*	kveða	kveð	kvað	kváðum	kveðinn
- *leak*	leka	lek	lak	lákum	lekinn
- *read*	lesa	les	las	lásum	lesinn
- *measure*	meta	met	mat	mátum	metinn
- *drive*	reka	rek	rak	rákum	rekinn
- *see*	sjá	sè	sá	sám	sènn
- *sleep*	sofa *or* svefa	sef	svaf	sváfum *or* sofum	sofinn
- *tread*	troða	treð	trað	tráðum	troðinn
- *weave*	vefa	vef	vaf, of	váfum, ofum	ofinn
- *fight*	vega	veg	vá	vágum, ogum	veginn

	inf.	pres.	pret. sing.	pret. plur.	past part.
to beg	biðja	bið	bað	báðum	beðinn
- lie	liggja	ligg	lá	lágum	leginn
- sit	sitja	sit	sat	sátum	setinn
- receive	þiggja	þigg	þá	þágum	þeginn
- bear	bera	ber	bar	bárum	borinn
- hide	fela	fel	fal	fálum	folginn
- come	koma	kem	kvam, kom	kvámum, komum	kominn
- take	nema	nem	nam	námum	numinn
- cut	skera	sker	skar	skárum	skorinn
- steal	stela	stel	stal	stálum	stolinn
- swim	svima, svema	svim, svam	svam	svámum	svominn.

Those verbs which have *v* before the vowel of the preterite sometimes take *ó* in the plural instead of *á*, generally with the dropt *v* as, *svófum* or *sófum*, *kvóðum* or *kóðum* for *sváfum* and *kváðum, vógum* for vágum, *ófum* for *váfum;* some have even *ó* in the singular, and thus inflect the preterite according to the third conjugation, namely, *óf, vó* = vaf, *vá*. The forms *kom*, plur. *kómum* from *koma*, are more common than *kvam* and *kvámum*.

Third Conjugation.

Vowel of the pret. *ó*, plur. *ó*.

Characteristics. — Simple root-consonant, excepting *vaxa;* vowel of the infinitive *a;* but when *j* is connected with the root-consonant *a* is changed into *é*, and the original *av* (*au*) into *ey*. Past part. *a;* but before *g* and *k* always *e*. Verbs in *eyj* have *á* in the past part. Those whose roots end in *g* reject that letter in the pret. sing., but take it again in the pret. plur. and past participle.

At fara *to journey.*

Indicative Mood.		Conjunctive Mood.	
Present.	Preterite.	Present.	Preterite.
I journey.	*I did journey.*	*I may journey.*	*I might journey.*
S. ek fer,	S. ek fór,	S. ek fari,	S. ek færi,
þú ferr,	þú fórð,	þú farir,	þú færir,
hann ferr;	hann fór;	hann fari;	hann færi;
P. ver förum,	P. vèr fórum,	P. vèr farim,	P. vèr færim,
þèr farið,	þèr fóruð,	þèr farið,	þèr færið,
þeir fara,	þeir fóru.	þeir fari.	þeir færi.

IMPERATIVE MOOD.		INFINITIVE MOOD.
far-ðu,	*do thou journey!*	at fara *to journey.*
förum,	*let us journey,*	*Pres. part.* farandi *journeying.*
farið,	*do ye journey.*	*Past part.* farinn *journeyed.*

To this conjugation belong the following verbs:

	inf.	pres.	pret. sing.	pret. plur.	past part.
to drive	aka	ek	ók	ókum	ekinn
- *feed*	ala	el	ól	ólum	alinn
- *die*	deyja	dey	dó	dóum, dóm	dáin
- *draw*	draga	dreg	dró	drógum	dreginn
- *flay*	flá	flæ	fló	flógum	fleginn
- *crow*	gala	gel	gól	gólum	galinn
- *bark*	geyja	gey	gó	góum	gáinn
- *dig*	grafa	gref	gróf	grófum	grafinn
- *heave*	hefja	hef	hóf	hófum	hafinn
- *laugh*	hlæja	hlæ	hló	hlógum	hleginn
- *lade*	hlaða	hleð	hlóð	hlóðum	hlaðinn
- *cut*	hnafa	hnef	hnóf	hnófum	hnafinn
- *souse*	kefja	kef	kóf	kófum	kafinn
- *freeze*	kala	kel	kól	kólum	kalinn
- *claw*	klæja	klæ	kló	klógum	kleginn
- *grind*	mala	mel	mól	mólum	malinn
- *scrape*	skafa	skef	skóf	skófum	skafinn
- *shake*	skaka, skekja	skek	skók	skókum	skekinn
- *shape*	skapa	skep	skóp	skópum	skapinn
- *strike*	slá	slæ	sló	slógum	sleginn
- *stand*	standa	stend	stóð	stóðum	staðinn
- *swear*	sverja	sver	sór	sórum	svarinn
- *take*	taka	tek	tók	tókum	tekinn
- *wade*	vaða	veð	óð	óðum	vaðinn
- *grow*	vaxa	vex	óx	óxum, uxum	vaxinn
- *wash*	þvá	þvæ	þvó, þó	þvógum	þveginn.

The imperative of *standa* is *stattu.*

FOURTH CONJUGATION.

Vowel of the pret. *ei*, plur. *i*.

Characteristics. — Root-vowel *i*; when the consonant *k* follows, *j* is inserted before the terminating *a* of the infinitive as, *vikja, svikja: biða* has the past part. *beðinn* for *biðinn*. Verbs, whose root is *ig*, form the pret. sing. in *è* instead of *eig*; for instance, stè = steig, hnè = hneig, sè = seig: this variation does not extend to the plural.

At grípa *to seize.*

INDICATIVE MOOD.		CONJUNCTIVE MOOD.	
Present.	Preterite.	Present.	Preterite.
I seize.	*I seized.*	*I may seize.*	*I might seize.*
S. ek grip,	S. ek greip,	S. ek gripi,	S. ek gripi,
þú gripr,	þú greipt,	þú gripir,	þú gripir,
hann gripr;	hann greip;	hann gripi;	hann gripi;
P. vèr gripum,	P. vèr gripum,	P. vèr gripim,	P. vèr gripim,
þèr gripið,	þèr gripuð,	þèr gripið,	þèr gripið,
þeir gripa.	þeir gripu.	þeir gripi.	þeir gripi.

IMPERATIVE MOOD.	INFINITIVE MOOD.
grip-ðu, *do thou seize;*	at grípa, *to seize.*
gripum, *let us seize,*	*Pres. part.* gripandi, *seizing.*
gripið, *do ye seize.*	*Past part.* gripinn, *seized.*

To this conjugation belong the following verbs:

	inf.	pres.	pret. sing.	pret. plur.	past part.
to bide	biða	bíð	beið	biðum	beðinn
- *bite*	bíta	bít	beit	bitum	bitinn
- *glitter*	blíka	blík	bleik	blikum	blikinn
- *drive*	drífa	drif	dreif	drifum	drifinn
- *yawn*	gína	gín	gein, ginda	ginum	gininn
- *sink down*	hníga	hníg	hneig, hnè	hnigum	hniginn
- *push*	hníta	hnít	hneit	hnitum	hnitinn
- *tear*	hrífa	hríf	hreif	hrifum	hrifinn
- *shriek*	hrína	hrín	hrein	hrinum	hrininn
- *whine*	hvína	hvín	hvein	hvinum	hvininn
- *climb*	klífa	klíf	kleif	klifum	klifinn
- *fear*	kvíða	kvíð, kvíði	kveið, kvidda	kviðum	kviðinn
- *glide on*	líða	líð	leið, lidda	liðum	liðinn
- *look at*	líta	lít	leit	litum	litinn
- *pass urine*	míga	míg	meig, mè	migum	miginn
- *ride*	ríða	ríð	reið	riðum	riðinn
- *tear in pieces*	rífa	ríf	reif	rifum	rifinn
- *rise*	rísa	rís	reis	risum	risinn
- *carve*	rista	rist	reist	ristum	ristinn
- *write*	ríta	rít	reit	ritum	ritinn
- *sink*	síga	síg	seig, sè	sigum	siginn
- *shine*	skína	skín	skein	skinum	skininn
- *step forth*	skríða	skríð	skreið	skriðum	skriðinn
- *slit*	slíta	slít	sleit	slitum	slitinn
- *cut*	sníða	sníð	sneið	sniðum	sniðinn
- *mount*	stíga	stíg	steig, stè	stigum	stiginn
- *scorch*	svíða	svíð	sveið, svidda	sviðum	sviðinn
- *flutter*	svífa	svíf	sveif	svifum	svifinn
- *betray*	svíkja	svík	sveik	svikum	svikinn
- *sweep*	svípa	svíp	sveip	svipum	svipinn
- *yield*	víkja	vík	veik	vikum	vikinn
- *lay hold of*	þrífa	þríf	þreif	þrifum	þrifinn.

Fifth Conjugation.

Vowel of the pret. *au* (*ó*), plur. *u*.

Characteristics. — Vowel of the infinitive *jó* before *t*, *ð*, *s*, *st*; but *jú* before *f*, *g*, *k*, *p*: *ú* in *lúta*, *lúka*, and sometimes *súga* for the more common form *sjúga*. Verbs, whose root is *júg*, form the pret. sing. in *ó* for *aug*, *e.g.* *smó* = *smaug*; *fló* = *flaug*; *ló* = *laug*; plur. always *smugum*, *flugum*, *lugum*.

At frjósa *to freeze.*

Indicative Mood.		Conjunctive Mood.	
Present.	Preterite.	Present.	Preterite.
I freeze.	*I froze.*	*I may freeze.*	*I might freeze.*
S. ek frýs,	S. ek fraus,	S. ek frjósi,	S. ek frysi,
þú frýst,	þú fraust,	þú frjósir,	þú frysir,
hann frýs;	hann fraus;	hann frjósi;	hann frysi;
P. vèr frjósum,	P. vèr frusum,	P. vèr frjósum,	P. vèr frysum,
þèr frjósið,	þèr frusuð,	þèr frjósið,	þèr frysuð,
þeir frjósa.	þeir frusu.	þeir frjósi.	þeir frysu.

Imperative Mood.	Infinitive Mood.
frjós-tu, *do thou freeze;*	at frjósa, *to freeze.*
frjósum, *let us freeze,*	*Pres. part.* frjósandi, *freezing.*
frjósið, *do ye freeze.*	*Past part.* frosinn, *frozen.*

To this conjugation belong the following verbs:

	inf.	pres.	pret. sing.	pret. plur.	past part.
to bid	bjóða	býð	bauð	buðum	boðinn
- *break*	brjóta	brýt	braut	brutum	brotinn
- *drop*	drjúpa	drýp	draup	drupum	dropinn
- *fly*	fljúga	flýg	flaug, fló	flugum	floginn
- *flow*	fljóta	flýt	flaut	flutum	flotinn
- *drift*	fjúka	fýk	fauk	fukum	fokinn
- *spurt*	gjósa	gýs	gaus	gusum	gosinn
- *pour*	gjóta	gýt	gaut	gutum	gotinn
- *obtain*	hljóta	hlýt	hlaut	hlutum	hlotinn
- *hammer*	hnjóða	hnýð	hnauð	hnuðum	hnoðinn
- *sneeze*	hnjósa	hnýs	hnaus	hnusum	hnosinn
- *knot*	hnjóta	hnýt	hnaut	hnutum	hnotinn
- *make bare*	hrjóða	hrýð	hrauð	hruðum	hroðinn
- *snore*	hrjóta	hrýt	hraut	hrutum	hrotinn
- *choose*	kjósa	kýs	kaus, kjöra	kusum, kurum	kosinn, korinn
- *cleave*	kljúfa	klýf	klauf	klufum	klofinn
- *creep*	krjúpa	krýp	kraup	krupum	kropinn
- *strike*	ljósta	lýst	laust	lustum	lostinn
- *lie*	ljúga	lýg	laug, ló	lugum	loginn
- *shut*	lúka	lýk	lauk	lukum	lokinn

	inf.	pres.	pret. sing.	pret. plur.	past part.
to stoop	lúta	lýt	laut	lutum	lotinn
- *enjoy*	njóta	nýt	naut	nutum	notinn
- *redden*	rjóða	rýð	rauð	ruðum	roðinn
- *destroy*	rjúfa	rýf	rauf	rufum	rofinn
- *smoke*	rjúka	rýk	rauk	rukum	rokinn
- *seethe*	sjóða	sýð	sauð	suðum	soðinn
- *suck*	sjúga, súga	sýg	saug, só	sugum	soginn
- *shoot*	skjóta	skýt	skaut	skutum	skotinn
- *slip away*	smjúga	smýg	smaug, smó	smugum	smoginn
- *stroke*	strjúka	strýk	strauk	strukum	strokinn
- *sip*	súpa	sýp	saup	supum	sopinn
- *pull*	tjúga	tý	taug, tó	tugum	toginn
- *fail*	þrjóta	þrýt	þraut	þrutum	þrotinn
- *roar*	þjóta	þýt	þaut	þutum	þotinn.

SIXTH CONJUGATION.

Vowel of the pret. è, plur. è.

Characteristics. — A single root-consonant after a long vowel, double after a short one: the vowel of the infinitive *ei* or *á* before a single, *a* before a double, consonant; vowel of the past part. like that of the inf., except in *ganga* and *fá*, where it is *e*.

At láta *to let.*

INDICATIVE MOOD.

Present. *I let.*	Preterite. *I did let.*
S. ek læt,	S. ek lèt,
þú lætr,	þú lèzt,
hann lætr;	hann lèt;
P. vèr látum,	P. vèr lètum,
þèr látið,	þèr lètuð,
þeir láta.	þeir lètu.

CONJUNCTIVE MOOD.

Present. *I may let.*	Preterite. *I might let.*
S. ek láti,	S. ek lèti,
þú látir,	þú lètir,
hann láti;	hann lèti;
P. vèr látim,	P. vèr lètim,
þèr látið,	þèr lètið,
þeir láti.	þeir lèti.

IMPERATIVE MOOD.

lát-tu, *do thou let;*
látum, *let us let,*
látið, *do ye let.*

INFINITIVE MOOD.

at láta, *to let.*
Pres. part. látandi, *letting.*
Past part. látinn, *let.*

To this conjugation belong the following verbs:

	inf.	pres.	pret. sing.	pret. plur.	past part.
to be called	heita	heit, heiti	hèt	hètum	heitinn
- *play*	leika	leik	lèk	lèkum	leikinn
- *swathe*	sveipa	sveip	svèp	svèpum	sveipinn
- *blow*	blása	blæs	blès	blèsum	blásinn
- *get*	fá	fæ	fèkk	fèngum	fenginn

	inf.	pres.	pret. sing.	pret. plur.	past part.
to weep	gráta	græt	grèt	grètum	grátinn
- *advise*	ráða	ræð	rèð	rèðum	ráðinn
- *mix*	blanda	blend	blètt	blèndum	blandinn
- *attire*	falda	feld	fèlt	fèldum	faldinn
- *go*	ganga	geng	gèkk	gèngum	genginn
- *hold*	halda	held	hèlt	hèldum	haldinn
- *hang*	hanga	heng	hèkk	hèngum	hanginn
- *fall*	falla	fell	fèll	fèllum	fallinn
- *sacrifice*	blóta	blœt	blèt	blètum	blótinn.

SEVENTH CONJUGATION.

Vowel of the pret. *jó*, plur. *jó*.

Characteristics. — Always a long root-syllable as the preceding, partly through a long vowel with a single consonant, partly by reason of position after a short vowel.

At ausa *to sprinkle.*

INDICATIVE MOOD.		CONJUNCTIVE MOOD.	
Present. *I sprinkle.*	Preterite. *I sprinkled.*	Present. *I may sprinkle.*	Preterite. *I might sprinkle.*
S. ek eys,	S. ek jós,	S. ek ausi,	S. ek jysi,
þú eyss,	þú jóst,	þú ausir,	þú jysir,
hann eyss;	hann jós;	hann ausi;	hann jysi;
P. vèr ausum,	P. vèr jósum, jusum,	P. vèr ausim,	P. vèr jysim,
þèr ausið,	þèr jósuð, jusuð,	þèr ausið,	þèr jysið,
þeir ausa.	þeir jósu, jusu.	þeir ausi.	þeir jysi.

IMPERATIVE MOOD.

aus, *do thou sprinkle;*
ausum, *let us sprinkle,*
ausið, *do ye sprinkle.*

INFINITIVE MOOD.

at ausa, *to sprinkle.*
Pres. part. ausandi, *sprinkling.*
Past part. ausinn, *sprinkled.*

To this conjugation belong the following verbs:

	inf.	pres.	pret. sing.	pret. plur.	past part.
to increase	auka	eyk	jók	jókum, jukum	aukinn
- *dwell*	búa	bý	bjó	bjoggum, bjuggum	búinn
- *leap*	hlaupa	hleyp	hljóp	hljópum, hlupum	hlaupinn
- *hew*	höggva	högg	hjó	hjoggum, hjuggum	höggvin
- *spew*	spýja	spý	spjó	spjóm	spúinn.

The words *búa* and *höggva* always shorten the vowel in the pret. plur.: *hlaupa, auka*, and *ausa* also become *hlupum, jukum*, and *jusum* in the same tense. These last two conjugations include those verbs which anciently formed the preterite by reduplication.

SECOND CLASS.

Sign-Forms.

Infinitive-ending *-a,* pret. sing. *-da* or *-di,* pret. plur. *-dum,* part. *-dr.* The connecting vowel is either *i* or *a:* this causes the division of verbs of this class (which answers to the German designation of *weak* verbs) into two conjugations.

First Conjugation.

With connecting vowel *i.*

The connecting vowel *i* always becomes *j* before another vowel: if *ji* come together a simple *i* takes their place.

There are two divisions of this conjugation according as the root-vowel is short or long. The *i* changed into *j*, is preserved in those verbs whose root-syllable is short as, temja *to tame,* vekja *to wake,* hylja *to hide,* and in fact in those which have a long syllable, but whose root ends in *g* and *k* as: vígja *to consecrate,* steikja *to roast,* byggja *to dwell.*

In the pret. and the past part. *d* remains unaltered after *l, m, n* in short-syllabled words.

First Division. Short root-vowel.

Verbs of this division have no final vowel in the pres. or in the pret. before the ending.

At telja *to reckon.*

Indicative Mood.		Conjunctive Mood.	
Present.	Preterite.	Present.	Preterite.
I reckon.	*I reckoned.*	*I may reckon.*	*I might reckon.*
S. ek tel,	S. ek taldi,	S. ek teli,	S. ek teldi,
þú telr,	þú taldir,	þú telir,	þú teldir,
hann telr;	hann taldi;	hann teli;	hann teldi;
P. vèr teljum,	P. vèr tõldum,	P. vèr telim,	P. vèr teldim,
þèr telið	þèr tõlduð,	þèr telið,	þèr teldið,
þeir telja.	þeir tõldu.	þeir teli.	þeir teldi.

Imperative Mood.

tel-du, *do thou reckon;*
teljum, *let us reckon,*
telið, *do ye reckon.*

Infinitive Mood.

at telja, *to reckon.*
Pres. part. teljandi *reckoning.*
Past part. taldr (taliðr, talinn), *reckoned.*

Thus are conjugated:

to choose velja	*to wean* venja	*to gladden* gleðja
- *dwell* dvelja	- *wake* vekja	- *whet* hvetja
- *beat* lemja	- *thatch* þekja	- *crave* krefja
- *smite* berja	- *take leave* kveðja	- *lead astray* glepja.

At hylja *to hide*.

Indicative Mood.		Conjunctive Mood.	
Present.	Preterite.	Present.	Preterite.
I hide.	*I hid.*	*I may hide.*	*I might hide.*
S. ek hyl,	S. ek huldi,	S. ek hyli,	S. ek hyldi,
þú hylr,	þú huldir,	þú hylir,	þú hyldir,
hann hylr;	hann huldi;	hann hyli;	hann hyldi;
P. vèr hyljum,	P. vèr huldum,	P. vèr hylim,	P. vèr hyldim,
þèr hylið,	þèr hulduð,	þèr hylið,	þèr hyldið,
þeir hylja.	þeir huldu.	þeir hyli.	þeir hyldi.

Imperative Mood.	Infinitive Mood.
hyl-du, *do thou hide;*	at hylja, *to hide.*
hyljum, *let us hide,*	*Pres. part.* hyljandi, *hiding.*
hylið, *do ye hide.*	*Past part.* huldr (huliðr, hulinn) *hidden.*

Thus are conjugated:

to ask spyrja	*to groan* stynja	*to roar* rymja
- *chew* tyggja	- *shut to* lykja	- *root out* ryðja.
- *carry* flytja	- *rush on* þysja	

Second Division. Long root-vowel.

Verbs of this division have the vowel *i* in the pres., but none in the pret. before the ending.

At dœma *to judge*.

Indicative Mood.		Conjunctive Mood.	
Present.	Preterite.	Present.	Preterite.
I judge.	*I judged.*	*I may judge.*	*I might judge.*
S. ek dœmi,	S. ek dœmdi,	S. ek dœmi,	S. ek dœmdi,
þú dœmir,	þú dœmdir,	þú dœmir,	þú dœmdir,
hann dœmir;	hann dœmdi;	hann dœmi;	hann dœmdi.
P. vèr dœmum,	P. vèr dœmdum,	P. vèr dœmim,	P. vèr dœmdim,
þèr dœmið,	þèr dœmduð,	þèr dœmið,	þèr dœmdið,
þeir dœma.	þeir dœmdu.	þeir dœmi.	þeir dœmdi.

Imperative Mood.	Infinitive Mood.
dœm-du, *do thou judge;*	at dœma, *to judge.*
dœmum, *let us judge,*	*Pres. part.* dœmandi, *judging.*
dœmið, *do ye judge.*	*Past part.* dœmdr, *judged.*

Thus are conjugated:

to deck prýða	*to follow* fylgja	*to fetch* heimta
- *make* gera	- *weaken* veikja	- *notice* geyma
- *gape* gapa	- *think* þeinkja	- *fell* fella
- *consecrate* vígja	- *spring* stökkva	- *drown* drekkja
- *sorrow* syrgja	- *speak* mæla	- *build* byggja.

SECOND CONJUGATION.

With connecting vowel *a*.

The connecting vowel *a* occurs in the preterite tense, and never falls away; but when *u* takes place in the inflections, it is changed into *u*, as:

	inf.	pret. sing.	pret. plur.	past part.
to love	elska	elskaði	elskuðum	elskadr
- *call*	kalla	kallaði	kölluðum	kallaðr.

At elska *to love*.

INDICATIVE MOOD.		CONJUNCTIVE MOOD.	
Present.	Preterite.	Present.	Present.
I love.	*I loved.*	*I may love.*	*I might love.*
S. ek elska,	S. ek elskaði,	S. ek elski,	S. ek elskaði,
þú elskar,	þú elskaðir,	þú elskir,	þú elskaðir,
hann elskar;	hann elskaði;	hann elski;	hann elskaði;
P. vèr elskum,	P. vèr elskuðum,	P. vèr elskim,	P. vèr elskaðim,
þèr elskið,	þèr elskuðuð,	þèr elskið,	þèr elskaðið,
þeir elska.	þeir elskuðu.	þeir elski.	þeir elskaði.

IMPERATIVE MOOD.

elska-ðu, *do thou love;*
elskum, *let us love,*
elskið, *do ye love.*

INFINITIVE MOOD.

at elska, *to love.*
Pres. part. elskandi, *loving.*
Past part. elskaðr, *loved.*

At kalla *to call*.

INDICATIVE MOOD.		CONJUNCTIVE MOOD.	
Present.	Preterite.	Present.	Preterite.
I call.	*I called.*	*I may call.*	*I might call.*
S. ek kalla,	S. ek kallaði,	S. ek kalli,	S. ek kallaði,
þú kallar,	þú kallaðir,	þú kallir,	þú kallaðir,
hann kallar;	hann kallaði;	hann kalli;	hann kallaði.
P. vèr köllum,	P. vèr kölluðum,	P. vèr kallim,	P. vèr kallaðim'
þèr kallið,	þèr kölluðuð,	þèr kallið,	þèr kallaðið'
þeir kalla.	þeir kölluðu.	þeir kalli.	þeir kallaði.'

IMPERATIVE MOOD.

kalla-ðu, *do thou call;*
köllum, *let us call,*
kallið, *do ye call.*

INFINITIVE MOOD.

at kalla *to call.*
Pres. part. kallandi, *calling.*
Past part. kallaðr, *called.*

The past participle in *-aðr* is regularly declined, as:

indef. kallaðr, kölluð, kallat
def. kallaði, kallaða, kallaða.

Like *kalla* are conjugated:

to serve þjóna	*to aim* ætla	*to gather* safna
- *plunder* herja	- *cast* kasta	- *prove* sanna
- *talk* tala	- *threaten* hóta	- *fall asleep* sofna
- *bake* baka	- *sound* hljóða	- *think* hugsa.
- *write* ríta		

PASSIVE VOICE.

The formation of the passive is very simple and regular: *st* is added in all cases, but before this, *r*, *t*, *d*, and ð are dropt, which last letter however takes *z* for *s*.

At teljast *to be reckoned.*	At dœmast *to be judged.*	At kallast *to be called.*

INDICATIVE MOOD.

Present.

I am reckoned.	*I am judged.*	*I am called.*
S. ek telst,	S. ek dœmist,	S. ek kallast,
þú telst,	þú dœmist,	þú kallast,
hann telst;	hann dœmist;	hann kallast;
P. vèr teljumst,	P. vèr dœmumst,	P. vèr köllumst,
þèr telizt,	þèr dœmizt,	þèr kallizt,
þeir teljast.	þeir dœmast.	þeir kallast.

Preterite.

I was reckoned.	*I was judged.*	*I was called.*
S. ek taldist,	S. ek dœmdist,	S. ek kallaðist,
þú taldist,	þú dœmdist,	þú kallaðist,
hann taldist;	hann dœmdist;	hann kallaðist;
P. vèr töldumst,	P. vèr dœmdumst,	P. vèr kölluðumst,
þèr tölduzt,	þèr dœmduzt	þèr kölluðuzt,
þeir töldust.	þeir dœmdust.	þeir kölluðust.

CONJUNCTIVE MOOD.

Present.

I may be reckoned.	*I may be judged.*	*I may be called.*
S. ek telist,	S. ek dœmist,	S. ek kallist,
þú telist,	þú dœmist,	þú kallist,
hann telist;	hann dœmist;	hann kallist;
P. vèr telimst,	P. vèr dœmimst,	P. vèr kallimst,
þèr telizt,	þèr dœmizt,	þèr kallizt,
þeir telist.	þeir dœmist.	þeir kallist.

Preterite.

I might be reckoned:	*I might be judged.*	*I might be called.*
S. ek teldist,	S. ek dœmdist,	S. ek kallaðist,
þú teldist,	þú dœmdist,	þú kallaðist,
hann teldist;	hann dœmdist;	hann kallaðist;
P. vèr teldimst,	P. vèr dœmdimst,	P. vèr kallaðimst,
þèr teldizt,	þèr dœmdizt,	þèr kallaðist,
þeir teldist.	þeir dœmdist.	þeir kallaðist.

IMPERATIVE MOOD.

telstu, *be thou reckoned;*	dœmstu, *be thou judged;*	kallastu, *be thou called;*
teljumst, *let us be reckoned,*	dœmumst, *let us be judged,*	köllumst, *let us be called,*
telizt, *be ye reckoned.*	dœmizt, *be ye judged.*	kallizt, *be ye called.*

INFINITIVE MOOD.

at teljast, *to be reckoned.*	at dœmast, *to be judged.*	at kallast, *to be called.*

Pres. participle.

teljandist, *being reckoned.*	dœmandist, *being judged.*	kallandist, *being called.*

Past participle.

talizt, *been reckoned.*	dœmizt, *been judged.*	kallazt, *been called.*

REFLECTIVE VERBS.

The passive voice is often expressed by the reflective form, which is thus constructed. To the verb active is appended the reflective pronoun *sik* (one's self), in the 1st pers. sing. *mik* (myself), the vowel being rejected; hence the 1st pers. sing. ends in *-mk,* the others have *-sk.*

The 1st pers. sing. adds *-mk* to the root of the verb through the connecting vowel *u,* as; from elska elsk-u-mk; from falla föll-u-mk; from bera bár-u-mk; sjámk *I look about me,* óumk *I fear,* vilnumk *I wish.*

The *-r* of inflection is dropt before -sk, as: 2. 3. pres. sing. dœmi-sk *for* dœmir-sk, skýt-sk *for* skýtr-sk.

The 1st pers. pl. is either formed like the 1st pers. sing., or it appends *-sk* to the ending *m,* thus, dœmumk *and* dœmumsk, skjótumk *and* skjótumsk.

According to these rules reflective verbs are thus conjugated:

at fallask, *to fall down.*	at skjótask, *to shrink.*	at fœðask, *to be nourished.*
	INDICATIVE MOOD.	
	Present.	
I fall down.	*I shrink.*	*I am nourished.*
S. ek föllumk,	S. skjótumk,	S. ek fœðumk,
þú fellsk,	þú skýtsk,	þú fœðisk,
hann fellsk;	hann skýtsk;	hann fœðisk;
P. vèr föllumsk, föllumk,	P. vèr skjótumsk, skjótumk,	P. vèr fœðumsk, fœðumk,
þèr falliðsk,	þèr skjótiðsk,	þèr fœðiðsk,
þeir fallask.	þeir skjótask.	þeir fœðask.
	Preterite.	
I fell down.	*I shrank.*	*I was nourished.*
S. ek fèllumk,	S. ek skutumk,	S. ek fœddumk,
þú fèllsk,	þú skautsk,	þú fœddisk,
hann fèllsk;	hann skautsk;	hann fœddisk;
P. vèr fèllumsk, fèllumk,	P. vèr skutumsk, skutumk,	P. vèr fœddumsk, fœddumk,
þèr fèlluðsk,	þèr skutuðsk,	þèr fœdduðsk,
þeir fèllusk.	þeir skutusk.	þeir fœddusk.

Examples: Sæll er sá er *stenzk* freistni, *happy he who withstands temptation;* bræðr munu *berjask,* ok at bönum *verðask, brothers will fight, and become each other's slayer;* öndin *fæðisk* ok *seðsk* (*sezk*) af guðligum málum, *the soul is nourished and satisfied with godly words;* vèr *hræðumsk* enn efsta dóm, *we fear the extreme sentence;* hugr misgeranda *snýsk* í örvilnan *the mind of ill-doers inclines to despair;* kona þín hefir *gipsk* þeim manni er hon kaus sèr *thy wife is married to the man whom she chose.*

ANOMALOUS VERBS.

I. Verbs having the characteristics of either class:

	inf.	pret. sing.	pret. plur.	past part.
to write,	ríta	reit	rítum	rítinn
or				
	rita	ritaða	rituðum	ritaðr.
- *worship,*	blóta	blèt	blètum	blótinn
or				
		blótaða	blótuðum	blótaðr.
- *mix,*	blanda	blètt	blèndum	blandinn
or				
		blandaða	blönduðum	blandaðr.

II. Verbs which have the characteristics of both conjugations in the second class, and which possess other irregularities:

	inf.	pres.	pret. ind. sing.	pret. conj.	past part.
to say	segja	segi	sagða	segða	sagðr
- *be silent*	þegja	þegi	þagða	þegða	þagat
- *think*	þykkja	þykki	þótta	þœtta	þótt
- *work*	yrkja	yrki	orta	yrta	ortr
- *seek*	sœkja	sœki	sótta	sœtta	sóttr
- *believe*	hyggja	hygg	hugða	hygða	hugaðr
- *will*	vilja	vil	vilda	vilda	viljaðr
- *set*	setja	set	setta	setta	settr
- *sell*	selja	sel	selda	selda	seldr
- *separate*	skilja	skil	skilda	skilda	skildr, skilinn
- *perform*	heyja, há	hái	háða	hæða	háðr
- *long for*	þreyja, þrá	þrái	þráða	þræða	þraðr
- *crush*	lýja	lý	lúða	lýða	lúðr, lúinn
- *flee*	flýja	flý	flýða	flýða	flýiðr
- *use*	duga	dugi	dugða	dygða	dugat
- *wake*	vaka	vaki	vakta	vekta	vakat
- *buy*	kaupa	kaupi	keypta	keypta	keyptr
- *endure*	þola	þoli	þolda	þylda	þolat
- *dare*	þora	þori	þorða	þyrða	þorat
- *put up with*	una	uni	unda	ynda	unat
- *live*	lifa	lifi	lifða	lifða	lifat
- *warn*	vara	vari	varða, varaða	verða	varat
- *believe*	trúa	trúi	trúða	trýða	trúaðr
- *reach*	ná	næ, nái	náða	næða	náðr
- *borrow*	ljá	lè, ljæ	lèða	lèða	lèðr, lènn
- *do*	gera, göra / görva	geri / göri	gerða / görða	gerða / görða	gerðr / görðr.

III. Verbs which have a peculiar irregularity:

to rub	gnúa	gný	gnèra	gnèri	gnúinn
- *turn*	snúa	sný	snèra	snèri	snúinn
- *row*	róa	ræ	rèra	rèri	róinn
- *grow*	gróa	græ	grèra	grèri	gróinn
- *sow*	sóa	sæ	sèra, sáða	sèri	sóinn, sáðr.

Slá *to strike*, a verb of the 1st class, 3rd conjugation, has also the pret. *slèra*.

IV. Anomalous verbs, mostly auxiliaries.

At eiga *to own, have.*

INDICATIVE MOOD.			CONJUNCTIVE MOOD.		
	I own.			*I may own.*	
Pres.	S. ek á,	P. vèr eigum,	Pres.	S. ek eigi;	P. vèr eigim,
	þú átt,	þèr eiguð,		þú eigir,	þèr eigið,
	hann á;	þeir eigu.		hann eigi;	þeir eigi.

Indicative Mood.		Conjunctive Mood.	
Preterite.		Preterite.	
I did own.		*I might own.*	
S. ek átta,	P. vèr áttum,	S. ek ætti,	P. vèr ættim,
þú áttir,	þèr attuð,	þú ættir,	þèr ættið,
hann átti;	þeir áttu.	hann ætti;	þeir ætti.
Pres. part. eigandi, *owning.*		*Past part.* áttr, *owned.*	

Thus are conjugated:

to be able, or, *to do* knega,
— — mega.

At kunna *to be able.*

Indicative Mood.		Conjunctive Mood.	
Present.		Present.	
I can, or, *am able.*		*I may be able.*	
S. ek kann,	P. vèr kunnum,	S. ek kunni,	P. vèr kunnim,
þú kant,	þèr kunnuð,	þú kunnir,	þèr kunnið,
hann kann;	þeir kunna.	hann kunni;	þeir kunni.
Preterite.		Preterite.	
I could, or, *was able.*		*I might be able.*	
S. ek kunna,	P. vèr kunnum,	S. ek kynni,	P. vèr kynnim,
þú kunnir,	þèr kunnuð,	þú kynnir,	þèr kynnið,
hann kunni;	þeir kunnu.	hann kynni;	þeir kynni.
Pres. part. kunnandi, *being able.*		*Past part.* kunnat, *been able.*	

Thus is conjugated:
to love, at unna.

At þurfa *to need.*

Indicative Mood.		Conjunctive Mood.	
Present.		Present.	
I need.		*I may need.*	
S. ek þarf,	P. vèr þurfum,	S. ek þurfi,	P. vèr þurfim,
þú þarft,	þèr þurfuð,	þú þurfir,	þèr þurfið,
hann þarf.	þeir þurfu.	hann þurfi;	þeir þurfi.
Preterite.		Preterite.	
I did need.		*I might need.*	
S. ek þurfta	P. vèr þurftum,	S. ek þyrfti,	P. vèr þyrftim,
þu þurftir	þèr þurftuð,	þú þyrftir,	þèr þyrftið,
hann þurfti;	þeir þurftu.	hann þyrfti;	þeir þyrfti.
Pres. part. þurfandi, *needing.*		*Past part.* þurft, *needed.*	

Skulu *shall, ought,* and munu *will, would,* irreg. inf.

INDICATIVE MOOD.

Present.

S. ek skal, þú skalt, hann skal;	P. vèr skulum, þèr skuluð, þeir skulu.
S. ek mun, man, þú munt, mant, hann mun, man;	P. vèr munum, þèr munuð, þeir munu.

Preterite.

S. ek skylda, munda, &c. | P. vèr skyldum, mundum, &c.
Part. *wanting*.

CONJUNCTIVE MOOD.

Present.

S. ek skuli, skyli, þú skulir, skylir, hann skuli, skyli;	P. vèr skulim, þèr skulið, þeir skuli.
S. ek muni, myni, þú munir, mynir, hann muni, myni;	P. vèr munim, þèr munið, þeir muni.

Preterite.

S. ek skyldi, myndi, &c. | P. vèr skyldim, myndim, &c.

The inf. form *skyldu*, and *mundu* is often found instead of *skulu* and *munu*.

At vita *to know*.

INDICATIVE MOOD.	CONJUNCTIVE MOOD.
Present.	Present.
I know.	*I may know.*
S. ek veit, P. vèr vitum, þú veitst, þèr vituð, hann veit; þeir vitu.	S. ek viti, P. vèr vitim, þú vitir, þèr vitið, hann viti; þeir viti.
Preterite.	Preterite.
I knew.	*I might know.*
S. ek vissa, &c. P. vèr vissum, &c.	S. ek vissi, &c. P. vèr vissim, &c.
Pres. part. vitandi, *knowing.*	*Past part.* vitat, *known.*

At muna *to remember* is, in nearly all its forms, conjugated like munu.

V. Verbs used variously:

þat berr við *it (sometimes) happens,*	hann skammast sín *he is ashamed of himself,*

ek forðask *I escape from my foes,*
mèr ofbýðr *I shudder,*
— verðr á *I make a mistake,*
— leiðist *I am weary,*
mik langtar *I long for,*
— þyrstir *I am thirsty,*
mik rekr *I am driven before the gale,*
— uggir *I am afraid of,*
mèr vill til *it happens to me,*
— heyrist *I hear,*
— skilsk *I understand.*

þèr tekst varla at *it will hardly be lucky for thee,*
þat tókst honum þó *it turned out lucky for him at last,*
— þrumar *it thunders,*
— dagar *it dawns;* and other verbs used impersonally.

CHAPTER VII.

UNINFLECTED WORDS.

PARTICLES.

Words which are mostly uninflected are classed under this denomination, as: adverbs, prepositions, conjunctions, and interjections.

CHAPTER VIII.

ADVERBS.

1. Of Place:

þar *there,*
hvar *where,*
hèr *here,*
út *out,*
inn *within,*
fram *forth, forward,*
ofan *above, down from above,*
þaðan *thence,*
hvaðan *whence,*
hèðan *hence,*
úti *abroad,*
innan *within, inside,*
neðan *down, below,*
braut *away,*
þaðra *thither,*
hvert *whither,*
hèðra *hither,*
útan *without, outside,*
innar *therein,*
uppi, upp *up, upwards,*
hvargi *nowhere.*

2. Of Time:

nú *now,*
timiliga *early,*
áðan *lately,*
þá *then,*
sjaldan *seldom,*
stundum *sometimes.*
fyrr *before,*
snemma *soon,*
lengi *long,*
enna *still, yet,*
tiðum *often,*
hèðanfrá *hereafter,*
síðla *late,*
hvenær *when,*
opt *often,*
forðum *formerly.*

3. Of Manner:

vel *well,*
gjarn *willingly,*
þanneg *in that way,*
illa *ill,*
svá *so,*
ágætliga *excellently.*
hverneg *how,*
sváleiðis *thus.*

4. Of Interrogation:

hversu *how*, hvat *what*, hvar *where*,
hvartill *whither*, hvarfyrir *wherefore*, hverninn *how*.

5. Of Affirmation:

já *yes*, vissulega *certainly*, sannlega *indeed*.

6. Of Negation:

nei *no*, eigi *not, by no means*.

CHAPTER IX.

PREPOSITIONS.

The prepositions mostly used are the following:

til *to*, af *of*, um *about*,
án *without*, frá *from*, á *on*,
auk *besides*, úr *out of*, í *in*,
ámilli *between*, undir *under*, með *with*,
fyrir *for*, mót *against*, við *by, at*,
að *at*, yfir *over*, eptir *after*.

CHAPTER X.

CONJUNCTIONS.

The conjunctions most in use are the following:

ok *and*,
bæði *both*,
sem *as*,
eðr — eðr *either — or*,
hvorki — nè *neither — nor*,
nè — nè *neither — nor*,
enn *than*,
en *but*,
annaðhvart — eða *either — or*,
því — því *the — the*,
utan *besides, but*,
ef *if*,
heldr enn *rather than*,
svá framarliga sem *so far as*,
nær *when*,
svá *so*,
ella *else*,
nema *if not, except*,
af því að *because*,
þótt *though*,
er *when*,
alls er *as, whereas, since*,
þá *when*,
þó *yet, although*,
þar eð *as*,
vegna þess að *on this account that*,
eins ok *as*,
enda þótt *although*.

CHAPTER XI.

INTERJECTIONS.

Some of the most common interjections are:

Ó! Hó! *alas!* Vel *well!* Gott ok vel *capital!* Bravo! and the like.

CHAPTER XII.

FORMATION OF WORDS.

The formation of words takes place through Derivation or Composition. In the former case it occurs through alteration of the inflection, change of vowel, or syllabic addition: in the latter case it arises from the junction of two or more separate words whose union forms a new one.

The original form of a word, and from which its derivations and inflections spring, is called the *root.* All roots are monosyllabic. A root by itself has no distinct meaning, but contains an idea which, in being developed, becomes the main idea of a family of kindred words. A root appears first in the form of a *verb,* because the first stage in the process of development is the idea of action or condition. All verbs, therefore, which come from a root by direct derivation, are called *radical* verbs.

By derivation is to be understood that increase which a word receives, and which is inserted between the root and the inflection, whereby the original idea is developed. Examples:

		Root.	Derivative.	Inflection.
to count	telja	tel	j	a
- *hew*	höggva	högg	v	a
cold	kaldr	kal	d	r
heaven	himinn	him	in	n.

Derivation is either vocalic (as transition of *i* into *j*, and of *u* into *v*, *see* tel-j-a, hög-v-a), consonantal (kal-d-r), or mixed; that is, consisting of vowel and consonant (him-in-n).

The vocalic Derivation.

In the vocalic derivation *i* (*j*) produces a vowel-change, and although itself dropt, is hereby known. Examples:

œði *madness,* from óðr *raging,*
bræði *passion,* — bráðr *hasty,*
ekra *ploughed land* — akr *field,*
byrðr (*dat. & acc.* byrði) *burden* from burðr *carrying,*
festr *rope,* from fastr *firm.*

The consonantal Derivation.

Every consonant-derivation appears originally to have been mixed, and when the vowel is lacking in Icelandic, it is often found in the cognate Teutonic tongues, as:

	Icelandic.	Old High German.		Icelandic.	Old High German.
old man	karl	charal	*laughter*	hlátr	hlahter
bird	fugl	fokal	*poison*	eitr	eiter
moon	tungl	zungel	*arm*	armr	aram
field	akr	achar	*thane*	þegn	degan
wakeful	vákr	wacker	*even*	jafn	ëban
finger	fingr	finkar	*raven*	hrafn	hraban.

CHAPTER XIII.

PREFIXES.

Afar- (Germ. *aber* in Aberglaube *superstition*) *highly, very greatly*: -auðigr *very rich*; -kostir *harsh conditions*; -ligr *of threatening appearance*; -menni *exceedingly strong man*; -orð *violent language*; -þungr *very heavy*.

Al- (from allr *all*) *quite, entirely*: -gjör *perfect*; -heill *quite hale*; -máttigr *almighty*; -mennr *general, public*; -menningr *the commonalty*; -vitr *all-wise*.

All- (*Lat. per* in *permultus*) *very, especially*: -gúþr *very brave*; -ríkr *very rich*; -stórr *very great*; -vel *very well*. This prefix answers to the English *right* or *very*.

And- *and* önd *against*: -nes *promontory opposite another at the month of a fjord*; -róðr *rowing against the wind*; -spænis *over against*; -styggiligr *abominable*; -viðri *contrary wind*; -sœlis *against the sun*; -streymis *against the stream*; -vígr *one who fights against*; öndverðr *fronting* (the opposite of ofanverðr *at the top*).

Auð- implies ease, and is opposed to *tor*: -fenginn *easily caught*; -fyndr *soon found*; -kenndr *easily known*; -næmr *soon apprehended*; -skilinn *easily understood*; -sóttr *easily gained*; -sær *soon discerned*; -trúa *credulous*.

Ein- *alone, extremely*: -harðr *courageous, bold*; -lægr *upright, sincere*; -seta *seclusion*.

Fjöl- (*Germ.* viel *much*, *Ang. Sax.* fela *many*, *Goth.* filu) *much, continual*: -bygðr *thickly-peopled*; -kynngi *great knowledge* (*witchcraft*); -menni *crowd*; -yrða *to be wordy*.

For- *before* (from the *prep.* fyrir): -faðir *forefather*; -máli *preface*; -ráð *supply*; -spár *foresight*; -streymis *with the stream*; -tölur *persuasions*; -vindis *with the wind*. It also conveys a notion of something dangerous or unpleasant, as in *Eng.* forlorn: forbænir *curses*; -dæma *to condemn*; -mæla *to curse*; -sending *dangerous mission*. It intensifies the meaning of verbs, as: forsmá *to scorn*.

Gagn- *quite opposite, through*: -hræddr *much frightened*; -læðr *very learned*; -mæli *contradiction*; -sær *transparent*; -staða *being opposite*.

Mis- has a negative meaning, and also implies dissimilarity, difference, or deterioration: -dauði *when one of two dies before the other*; -grip *mistake*; -jafn *uneven*; -kaup *bad purchase*; -líka *to dislike*; -litr *pied*; -skilningr *misunderstanding*; -þyrma *to ill-treat*.

Sam- (from saman *together*): -borgarmaðr *co-citizen*; -borinn *born of the same parents*; -dœgris *on the same day*; -fagna *to rejoice with one*; -feðra *having the same father*; -nafni *having the same name as another*; -þykki occurrence.

Sí- *continual, uninterrupted*: -byrðr *lying alongside* (*of ships*); -felldr *continuous*; -máll *always prating*. This word occurs in the phrase sí ok æ *ever and aye*.

Sjald- (from sjaldan) *seldom*: -gætr *seldom obtained*; sènn *seldom seen*.

Sundr- (opposite of *sam*) *asunder*: -mæðr *having another mother*; -þykki *disunion*.

Tor- implies difficulty: -breytiligr *hard to manage*; -fyndr *bad to find*; -færa *bad travelling*; -gætr *difficult to get*; -næmr *dull-witted*; -tryggr *distrustful*.

Ú- *or* ó- is a negative particle, mostly used before adjectives, and answers to the Eng. *un*: -friðr *discord*; -hóf *excess*; -kunnr *unknown*; -mak *uneasiness*; -missandi *indispensable*; -sjaldan *often*.

Van- implies want, fault: -færr *unable*; -gá *carelessness*; -heilsa *sickliness*; -trú *unbelief*.

Ör- (er-) has a privative signification: erlendis *abroad*; -lítill *very little*; -mjór *very thin*; -viti *foolish*.

CHAPTER XIV.

AFFIXES.

-a: by this ending adjectives are mostly formed into adverbs as, gjarna *willingly* (from gjarn), illa *badly* (illr), and viða *widely* (viðr). It likewise forms many indeclinable adjectives, as afsinna *mad*, landflótta *exiled*.

-aldi has a deteriorative meaning, as: glópaldi *simpleton*; þumbaldi *a peevish fellow*.

-alt, -ilt, -ult, -lt shows a state or quality as: gamalt *old*; sannsögult *truthful*.

-an is an adverbial termination, as: áðan *lately*, meðan *meanwhile*. It mostly means motion from a place, as: hèðan *hence*.

-ari is mostly used of persons, as: skrifari *writer*, though sometimes of things.

-at, to a place: hingat *hither*, þangat *thither*.

-dagi: bardagi *battle*, skildagi *contract*.

-dómr: konungdómr *kingdom*, vísdómr *wisdom*.

-erni forms neuter substantives indicating kinship: bróðerni *brotherhood*, faðerni *fatherhood*, líferni *way of living*.

-fræði answers to Eng. *lore*: fornfræði *antiquities*, guðfræði *theology*, málfræði *grammar* (*speech-lore*).

-ill forms diminutives: bleðill *leaflet*, kistill *a small chest*.

-ing, a feminine termination: drottning *queen*, kerling *crone*.

-ingi, used of persons: erfingi *heir*, heiðingi *heathen*.

-ingr, used of natives of countries which end in *ey*, as Færeyíngr *a Faroese*, Orkneyíngr *an Orkneyan*.

-la, a feminine diminutive corresponding with -ill, -ull: hrísla *a twig*, pyttla *a small pot*.

-látr signifies disposition or quality of the mind: rèttlátr *righteous*, þrálátr *wilful*.

-læti, formed from adjectives in -látr: lauslæti *frivolity*, ranglæti *unrighteousness*.

-leitr refers mostly to bodily appearance: hvítleitr *whitish*, rauðleitr *ruddy*.

-leysi from adjectives in laus: sakleysi (Provincial Eng. *sackless*, *i. e. simple*) *innocence*, vitleysi *folly*.

-ligr means *like* (Eng. *-ly, like*): höfðingligr *princely*, hetjuligr *hero-like*.

-lingr forms diminutives. bæklingr *a little book*, yrmlingr *a wormling*. It also forms patronymics, as Knýtlingr (from Knútr *Canute*), Ynglingr (from Yngvi).

-na forms the ending of many inceptive verbs: blikna *to turn pale*, hitna *to grow hot*, kólna *to cool*. It also intensifies the meaning of adverbs: hèrna *just here*, núna *just now*.

-naðr *or* -nuðr: búnaðr *appurtenances*, mánuðr *month*.

-neyti *fellowship*, from nouns in -nautr: föruneyti *fellow-traveller*, mötuneyti *messmate*.

-ni forms feminine substantives from adjectives in -inn: forvitni *curiosity*, hlýðni *obedience*.

-óttr implies an outward form: dropóttr *in form of drops*, kringlóttr *spherical*.

-ra: haltra *to halt*, hliðra *to yield*.

-rœnn denotes a district: austrœnn *from the east*, fjallrœnn *from the fells*. Hence some feminine substantives, as norrœna *the north wind, the Norse language*.

-sa: glepsa *to snatch at*, hramsa *to seize*.

-si: bersi *bear*, gassi *goose*, ofsi *pride*. This ending is rare.

-ska signifies a quality: fólska *silliness*, mælska *talkativeness*.

-skr terminates many proper adjectives: enskr *English*, gauzkr *Gothic*, íslenzskr *Icelandic*.

-sl: beisl *bit*, hermsl *sorrow*, kynsl *strange event*.

-sla: fœzla *maintenance*, geymsla *care*, vígsla *consecration*.

-ta renders transitive: lykta *to shut*, neita *to deny*, skemta *to joke*.

-und: tegund *species*, vitund *knowledge*, þúsund *thousand*.

-usta *or* -osta: fullusta *satisfaction*, þjónusta *service*.

-verðr (Eng. *wards*): austanverðr *eastward*, utanverðr *outward*.

-ynja forms a few feminine nouns: apynja *she-ape*, ásynja *goddess*, vargynja *she-wolf*.

CHAPTER XV.

COMPOSITION.

Composition means the forming of one word out of two or more, with or without change of form in either. Of these, the last is considered as the chief word; the first serves to define it more closely, as: bogmaðr *bowman*, sækonungr *sea-king*, hárfagr *fair-haired*, kennimaðr *pastor*.

In words framed by composition, each of the constituents may possess, and still retain, an independent significance, as for example, in *steam-boat*, in which instance each of the words has just the same sense as when employed by itself, though, in order to complete the meaning of the compound something must be understood. In the majority of compound words, the component parts are not all separately significant, but the word consists of a principal radical, the sense of which is reversed, extended, limited, or otherwise qualified, by combining with it a particle or other determinative, not of itself expressive of a state, quality, or act.

Composition of Nouns.

Nominal composition is either proper or improper. It is proper when the first word rejects all inflection, and its root alone is joined to the following, as: bogmaðr *bowman*, jarðhús *underground house*, *cell*, mjöðdrekka *mead vessel*, eldhús *brew-house*, blóðfall *flow of blood*. In such cases the constituents cannot be separated, but must necessarily be included under one idea.

Nominal composition is improper, when its first member is placed in the genitive, as: konungsmaðr *king's man*, hjartarhorn *hartshorn*, sonardóttir *granddaughter*, konuríki *female rule*, eyrnaverkr *earache*, ennisbreiðr *having a broad forehead*, herðabreiðr *broad-shouldered*; where the two members could also be written separately and regarded as two words. Sometimes the mode in which the compound is framed considerably affects its signification; thus, konungmaðr *a royal person*, is much the same as konungr, but konungsmaðr on the contrary, a man who is in the king's service.

Feminines in *-i*, which are indeclinable in the singular, and stand first in composition, are sometimes connected with the following member by *s*, as: frændsemis-talr *genealogical enumeration*, hræsnis-ligr *hypocritical*, úgleðis-klæði *mourning-clothes*. These compounds resemble the German *Liebesbrief*.

Composition of Adjectives.

Here the first adjective mostly takes the same changes as the same member in compound substantives.

Many adjectives are composed of two others, the last being always the chief word, as: sannheilagr *truly holy*, stórgjöfull *open-handed*, lauslyndr *fickle*. The last part of some compounds is a substantive which takes an adjectival form in consequence of the composition, as: þríhöfðaðr *three-headed*, langorðr *wordy*, rangeygðr *squint-eyed*, fagrhærðr *fair-haired*, skammlífr *short-lived*.

The adjective is placed last in the following and similar compounds: hálslangr *long-necked*, svíradigr *thick-necked*, smekkgóðr *good-tasted*, nefmikill *big-nosed*, skiðfœrr *able to run with snow-shoes*. Thus the participles are always placed last, as: fótbrotinn *broken-legged*, sóttbitinn *natural death*, ryðgenginn *rust-eaten*, járnsleginn *iron-shod*.

Composition of Verbs.

Adverbs and prepositions are frequently compounded with verbs, as: aftaka *to beat off*, útreka *to drive out*, upptaka *to take up*, fráskilja *to separate*, which may be written with equal correctness *taka af*, *upp*, *reka út*, *skilja frá*.

When a substantive is compounded with a verb the latter constitutes the last part of the composition, as: krossfesta *to crucify*, handhöggva *to cut off the hand*, fótfara *to measure by the step*, lífláta *to put to death*, lögtaka *to accept as law*, auglýsa *to make plain*, varðveita *to keep guard*, fóttroða *to tread under foot*.

When the verb forms the first part of the compound its infinitive sign is often dropt, being supplied by the vowel *i* which connects it with the remaining member of the compound, as: kennimaðr *priest*, lærifaðir *teacher*, lærisveinn *disciple*, rennismiðr *turner*, sendiboði *messenger*, spennitöng *pincers*.

Verbs compounded with adjectives are rare; the following are examples: ranglýsa *to state incorrectly*, sannfœra *to persuade*, kunngöra *to announce*.

Words chiefly used as Compounds.

1. As the first compound member are used

Einka- *own, proper, peculiar:* einkagrípr *costly jewel,* -leyfi *privilege,* -mál *secret discourse,* -vinr *confidential friend.* This word must not be confounded with einga *single.* It is a feminine substantive in the genitive, but is used only in genitives plural in composition to give the following member the signification of something special.

Endr- *again:* -bót *reform,* -gjald *repayment,* -lausn *redemption.*

Fá- *few:* -kunnig *ignorant,* -mennr *having few folk,* -vizka *deficient understanding.*

Fer- *or* fjór- *four:* -faldr *fourfold,* -hyrndr *four-cornered,* -nættingr *four days old.*

Frum -*original:* -burðr *first-born,* -getinn *first-begotten,* -móðir *original parent,* -rit *original writing.* This word is the Gothic and Anglo-Saxon frum *beginning.*

Full- *full:* -dimmr *quite dark,* -gamall *very old,* -hugi *courageous.*

Góð- *good:* -fúss *benevolent,* -menni *a brave man,* -viðri *good weather.*

Höfuð- *head, chief:* -engill *archangel,* -gæfa *chief luck,* -prestr *high-priest.*

Ill- *bad:* -fúss *malicious,* -gerð *outrage,* -gresi *weed.*

Ný- *new:* -kominn *just come,* -lenda *newly-tilled land,* -mæli *news.*

Of- *much of:* -át *gluttony,* -gamall *much too old,* -mikill *too great,* -seinn *too late.*

Ofr- shows a high degree: -efli *superior force,* -máta *exceedingly.*

Smá- *small,* forms diminutives: -konungr *petty king,* -kvikendi *small cattle,* -mey *little girl,* -sveinn *little boy.*

Stór- *great,* forms augmentatives: -auðigr *very rich,* -eign *large property,* -illa *very ill,* -rikr *very rich.*

Tví- *two:* -bura *twin sisters,* -drœgni *discord,* -fœttr *two-legged.*

Þjóð-, has an intensive meaning: -gata *high-road,* -konungr *chief-sovereign,* -skáld chief bard.

2. As the last compound member are used

-**borg**, which is often added to the name of a town: Athenuborg *Athens,* Jórsalaborg *Jerusalem.*

-dœmi: biskupsdœmi *bishoprick*, einvaldsdœmi *monarchy*, hertogadœmi *dukedom*.

-efni one who will become something: konungsefni *crown-prince*, mágsefni *future brother-in-law*.

-gjarn shows desire: fégjarn *covetous*, hólgjarn *fond of flattery*, metnaðargjarn *ambitious*, námgjarn *studious*, þrætugjarn *fond of strife*.

-kona *woman*: einsetukona *female hermit*, þjónustukona *handmaid*.

-korn forms diminutives: hópkorn *a small heap*, karlkorn *a little man*, piltkorn *a little boy*, ritkorn *a small writing*.

-land, often appended to the name of a country: Indialand, Polinaland, Prussaland.

-lauss, a negative, answering to the English *-less*: huglauss *spiritless*, konunglaust *interregnum*, vápnlauss *weaponless*.

-list *art*: skáldskaparlist *the poetic art*, þrætulist *argumentative skill*.

-maðr *man*: gleðimaðr *a lively man*, mælskumaðr *an eloquent man*.

-menni: góðmenni *a brave man*, illmenni *a bad man*, lítilmenni *an insignificant man*, mikilmenni *a famous man*. This word occurs only in composition.

-víss shows quality: daunvíss *keen-scented*, hvatvíss *headlong*, lævíss *cunning*, stelvíss *thievish*.

PART III.

SYNTAX.

CHAPTER I.

OF NOUNS, ADJECTIVES, AND PRONOUNS.

In Icelandic, as in other languages, an adjective agrees in number, gender, and case with the substantive which it qualifies. Even in substantives which, with a masculine or neuter form, have a feminine signification, and with a feminine or neuter form have a masculine one, there is no exception to this rule, as the adjective in these cases takes the grammatical, not the real, gender. Thus, hitt fagra víf (*neut.*) *the fair woman*, friðr svanni (*masc.*) *a handsome woman*, flagðit ljóta (*neut.*) *the loathsome sorceress*, greyit litla (*neut.*) *the little dog*, hann var skáld gott (*neut.*) *he was a good poet*, hann var hetja mikil (*fem.*) *he was a great champion*.

Many masculine and neuter nouns with a feminine signification are poetical names of women as, svarri, svanni, sprund, fljóð. Of neuters with a masculine signification are most compound words in menni, as: ungmenni, mikilmenni, afarmenni. Yet when the person thus signified is mentioned immediately afterwards, it is in the natural gender, as: sá ek þá hina miklu hetju (*fem.*); hann var friðr sýnum *then I saw that great champion; he was of fair countenance:* rœdda ek við fegrstan svanna (*masc.*); hon er kvenna kurteisust *I spoke to the fairest woman; she is the most courteous of women.*

Titles mostly follow the proper name, as: Haraldr konungr *King Harald*, Sigurðr jarl *Earl Sigurðr*. Asvaldr hertogi *Duke Oswald*, Otto keisari hinn mikli *the emperor Otto the Great*, Ari prestr *Priest Ari*, Krístina drottning *Queen Christina*.

Herra and Síra (*Sir*), Frú, Madame (*Madam*), Frúken and Jungfrú (*Miss*), however, precede the name. Herra *lord, master*, applies to kings, bishops, and knights; Síra is used only of priests, a title answering to our word *sire*, that is, *Father*, which mode of addressing their clergy is still common amongst the Scandinavian peasantry, and formerly prevailed in England, as we meet with "Sir Parson" in old writings. When substantives which denote some member of a person, show that the action which the sentence describes, concerns more the person than the particular member, the person takes the dative, *e. g.*, hann fèll fram á fœtr konungi *he fell forward at the king's feet.* On the other hand, when the action refers to the bodily parts themselves the genitive is used, as: þvær hann fœtr konungs *he washes the king's feet.* In the same manner the dative of the personal pronoun is used instead of the possessive, *e. g.*, leysti hann bönd af fótum sèr *he loosed the fetters from his feet*, not fótum sínum, as the release was not confined to the feet, but affected the whole body.

When an adjective or pronoun refers to two substantives one of which is masculine, the other feminine, it takes the neuter, *e. g.*, þat kveld gèkk hann at bruðlaupi með Brynhildi, en er *þau* (*neut.*) kómu í sæing, þá dró hann sverðit fram or sliðrum ok lagði í millum þeirra *that evening he wedded Brynhildur; but when they got into bed, he drew his sword out of the sheath, and placed it between them:* vit (Loki ok Freyja) skolum aka *tvau* (*neut.*) *we two* (*Loki and Freyja*) *shall drive:* mælti *hvárt* við *annat* (*neut.*) *they spoke to one another* (of a man and woman): ef bóndi mælir at kona skal barn sitt af brjósti sèr láta, ok hefir hann kvánríki svá mikit, at hon vill eigi at orðum hans láta, þá er hon sek mörkum 3 af sínu einu fè; en ef hann gár eigi heldr en hon, þá eru *þau bæði* sek mörkum af beggja þeirra fè, *if a peasant says that his wife must wean her child, and he is so much henpecked that she will not heed his words, then is she finable in 3 marks of her own money; but if he cares no more about it than she does, then are they both subject to a mulct in marks of the money of both:* enn er *þau* (Grímr ok Lopthæna) vóru búin, ok byr gaf, hèldu þau tveim skipum austr með landi, *but when they* (*Grímr and Lopthæna*) *were ready, and a fair breeze sprung up, they steered their two ships eastwards along the coast.*

From the same reason the substantives feðgin *father and daughter,* mœðgin *mother and son,* systkin *brother and sister* are neuter, as each word signifies persons of different sex.

When several proper names are connected by the conjunction *ok*, the personal pronoun is usually added, especially when the names so joined form the subject of the sentence, *e. g.,* þau Björgólfr ok Hildiríðr áttu 2 sonu, *Björgólfr and Hildiríðr had 2 sons;* eptir þat fóru þeir Sigurðr ok Reginn á Gnýtaheiði *afterwards Sigurðr and Reginn went to Gnyta heath.* Börn þeirra váru þau Gunnarr, Högni, Guðrún, Guðný, *their children were Gunnarr,* &c. The pronoun, however, is often omitted when all the persons are feminine, as: þat var eitt sinn at Brynhildr ok Guðrún gengu til vatns at bleikja hadda sína *once it chanced that Brynhildr and Gudrún went to the river to wash their hair* (not *þær Brynhildr ok Guðrún*).

The conjunction *and* is frequently omitted before a proper noun preceded by a personal pronoun, when the latter takes the dual or plural number in the same case as the proper noun, as: geri ek hin þriðju manngjöld fyrir fjörráð við *ykkr Þóri I adjudge the third fine for the plot against thee and Thórir.* If *yðr Þóri* had stood here, the translation would have been *you and Thórir*. Eyjólfr var opt við skip um sumarit, ok áttu þeir Hreiðvarr mart saman í vinfengi, *Eyjólfr was often on his ship in summer time, and he and Hreiðvarr were bosom friends*. Nú er þórólfr þar í allmiklum kærleikum af konungi, ok báðir þeir Bárðr, *now is Thórólfr much in the king's favour, and both he and Bárdr*; vinátta *okkar Hákonar* konungs stendr grunnt, *King Hákon's friendship and mine is not well-grounded*; þau Kveldúlfr áttu 2 sonu, *Kveldúlfr and his wife had two sons*. The context alone often determines which persons are signified by the pronoun, for *þau Kveldúlfr* could also mean *Kveldúlfr and the other women*, or, *Kveldúlfr and the other men and women*. Thus: nú ríða þeir þráinn ofan frá Dal *now ride Thráinn and the others* (seven persons are here alluded to) *down from Dal*. When the proper noun stands in the genitive, the possessive is placed instead of the genitive of the personal pronoun in the 1st and 2nd person in the same case as the substantive to which it relates, as: sammæli *okkart* þrándar *the covenant between me and Thrandr*; fundr várr Bagla *the meeting between me and the Bagla folk*. Before proper nouns *hann* or *hon* is often placed superfluously, as: hann Ólafr, *i. e.* Ólafr. If no person be named to whom the pronoun can refer, *þeir* in the plural agreeing in case with a proper noun in the singular, forms an idiom exactly expressing the Greek *οἱ περί* with a noun*, as: þeir Sigurðr lögðu fram, *Sigurdr and he set forward*; þeim Hákoni byrjaði seint *Hakon and he got a fair wind late*.

The definite article *hinn, hin, hit* is also written *inn, in, it, enn, en, et,* and can be used postpositively (see p. 14). In modern Icelandic *sá, sú, þat* is used instead of *hinn* as an article; in Old Norse it is demonstrative; thus, sá góði konungr must not be translated "the good king", but "this", or "that good king", and properly should be expressed sá hinn góði konungr. A word may take the article both before and after it, as: sáttu þann hinn mikla manninn, *didst thou see that great man?* or þann hinn mikla mann?

When an adjective follows a substantive used in the definite form, either of the following modes of expression

* *οἱ περὶ Ἄνυτον Anytus*, or, *Anytus with his companions*. The French use *nous autres* in a similar way; for instance, nous autres Français, *we Frenchmen*, conveying the idea "I and all other Frenchmen".

may be adopted. konungrinn ríki, (*i. e.*, konungr hinn ríki) or, konungrinn hinn ríki, *the rich king*.

Occasionally the article *hinn* is omitted, and the adjective used indefinitely along with the substantive, especially with proper nouns, as: dalr mikli (for *hinn mikli*), Mikligarðr (hinn mikli garðr), Langavatn (hit langa vatn), Hákon konungr góði *King Hákon the Good*, Saga Harallds harðráða *the history of Haralldr Harðráði*.

The possessive pronoun *sinn* is used when reference is made to the subject of the verb, as: hann hefir sinn hatt *he has his* (*own*) *hat*; but *hann hefir hans hatt* would mean, *he has his* (*another's*) *hat*. þeir tóku sína hatta *they took their* (*own*) *hats*; þeir tóku þeirra hatta *they took their* (*other persons'*) *hats*.

Partitives, as well superlative adjectives and numerals, as pronouns, also govern the genitive, as: hann var allra skálda mestr *he was the greatest of all bards*; hverr þeirra hefir þat gert *which of them has done that?*; ek veit eigi hvárt nokkurr várr mundi *I know not whether any of us will*; þá blótaði hann, ok lifði hann þá enn tíu vetra *then he sacrificed, and still lived ten years*. The adjectival partitive takes the neuter singular, as: mart manna *many men*.

When the genitives *vár, ykkar, yðar* are governed by a partitive or pronoun, the corresponding possessives *várr, ykkarr, yðarr* are used instead of them in apposition with the word which governs the genitive, as: drepa mun hann einn várr, *he must kill one of us*; engi várr (*nemo noster* for *nemo nostrúm*), *none of us*; engum várum bræðrum *to none of us brothers*, hverr várr þriggja *each of us three*.

When the reciprocal pronoun *sjálfr* in the genitive, connected with a possessive, expresses our *own*, the possessive always answers in case, gender, and number to *sjálfr* and not to the word which governs it in the genitive, as: í sjálfs þíns kapellu, *in thy own sacristy*; at sjálfra várra vilja, *according to our own will*; fyrir sál sjálfrar sinnar, *for her own soul*.

The interrogative pronoun *hvat* (Germ. *was für*, Dan. *hvad for*), *what kind of*, has generally the dative after it, more rarely the genitive, *e. g.* hon spurði hvat manni hann var, *she asked what kind of man he was*; hvat þröng er þat, *what crowd is that?* prestr spurði, hvat sukki þar væri, *the priest asked, what was the row*; hvat manna, *what kind of men?*

The dative is used:

1. without a preposition when a word denotes a means, instrument, or manner: hon var troðin hestafótum til bana, *she was trodden under foot of horses to death;* hann mælir feigum munni *he speaks with a dying mouth;* var þat eiðum bundit, *that was confirmed by oaths;* hann varð því feginn *he was glad of it;* hon var fríð sýnum, *she had a fair countenance;* hann hèt svá öðru nafni, *he was thus called by another name:*

2. where a word stands as a definitive with some comparative, preposition or adverb: hon var miklu fríðari en þóra, *she was much fairer than Thóra;* hálfum mánuði seinna *half a month later;* tveim örtugum minna en eyrir *two-thirds less than an ounce;* Hemíngr andaðist vetri síðar *Hemíngr died the winter after;* árum eptir Nóa flóð *the year after Noah's flood:*

3. where a word defines or intensifies the comparative: hann var hverjum manni sterkari *he was stronger than any man;* hverri konu fegri *fairer than any woman;* dökkálfar eru svartari biki *the swart elves are darker than pitch:*

4. when the preposition *at* is employed with the comparative (sometimes instead of *því*), as: menn voru þeir *at* vaskari, *they were men so much the braver;* engi maðr mun Erík kalla *at* meira konung þó at hann drepi einn bóndason, *no man will call Erik a king any more for slaying a peasant's son:*

5. or with a participle when it answers to the Greek genitive absolute and the Latin ablative absolute: *at* því görvu (*hoc facto*), *this being done;* *at* uppverandi sólu, *whilst the sun was shining;* yet *at* is sometimes omitted.

In order to indicate length of time or distance, the substantive which defines either is placed in the accusative, as: dvaldist hann þar mörg misseri *he abode there many years;* þeir fóru átta rastar *they travelled eight miles;* fara land veg, sjóleiðina *to go by land, by sea;* þann veg *that way;* marga lund *many ways.* Exception: hann fór leiðar sinnar (*gen.*), *he went on his way;* thus the Germ. *er zog seines Weges.*

When in a phrase a substantive or pronoun is to stand in a dependent relation (either governed by a preposition or the verb itself), it is sometimes introduced into a proposition which begins with *þar sem, þar er,* and becomes the subject of it: hafði erkibiskupinn þar mikit at styðjast við, sem Jón var, *the archbishop had much to rely upon where Jón was, i. e.,* found firm support in him; mun nú ekki þurfa at ætla til sæmdar, þar sem hann er *it cannot now avail to expect any honour where he is, i. e.,* on his part, from him; kom þat ok þar fram, er Þorsteinn var, *this also happened where Thorsteinn was,* it struck Thorsteinn also; muntu þykkjast litlu til verja, þar sem ek em, *thou thinkest indeed that thou sacrificest little where I am, i. e.,* by sacrificing me.

Expressions such as *við* or *með tólfta mann* do not mean "with twelve men", but "myself the twelfth with eleven others", or "with eleven others"; therefore when we find the ordinal expressed in the same way as the cardinal number, namely by cyphers, *e. g.,* við XII mann, the vowel in *mann* can alone determine the correct translation: við XII menn would signify "with 12 men".

Genitives and possessives are mostly placed before their corresponding nouns when used emphatically; but otherwise after them, as: gerðu þat fyrir hennar sakar! *do that for her sake.* Bróðir hans var kominn áðr, *his brother had come before;* er þeir fundu Gunnhildi móður sína, *when they found Gunnhildur their mother.*

When one noun denotes a part of another, or rather helps to modify it, the name of the substance must precede, and be compounded with the other word; but if not a noun, or incapable of composition, the name of the substance must follow with the preposition *af,* as: hann kastaði kökubita fyrir hundinn *he threw a bit of cake to the dog,* af barkarstykkjum þeim *from the pieces of bark;* korntunnan kostar 20 r. dr., *a tun of rye costs* 20 *rix dollars;* lítið af saffrani *a little saffron.*

The indefinite and definite form of adjectives may be used interjectionally, as: karl minn góðr, *my good fellow!* barnit gott, *the good child!* húsmóðir góð, *good housewife!* ek vilda, góðr drengr, at þú gengir inn í stofuna, *I wish thee, good lad, to go into the room.* Nú, Jón litli! piltr litli, *now, little John, little boy.* But the sense becomes collective when both the substantive and adjective are put in the definite form, as: góða barnit, *the good child,* or, *good children.*

When adjectives signify measure they take the name of

the measure in the genitive, as: hálfrar annarrar álnar langr, *an ell and a half long,* þrjátíu ára gamall *thirty years old.*

The indefinite pronouns *one another,* and *the one — the other,* are mostly expressed by the simple passive or reflective form of the verb, as: er þeir vóru búnir, hlaupast þeir at, *when they were equipped, they ran one against the other;* Pýramus ok Tisbe þau unnust, *Pyramus and Thisbe loved each other.*

Every other, every third year, is expressed in an inverted order, *e. g.,* annat, þriðja, fjórða, hvert ár. This is the case likewise with the article, *e. g.,* at hvíla hinn sjöunda hvern dag, *to rest every seventh day;* hit tíunda hvert ár *every tenth year.*

Hálft (the Germ. *halb*) precedes the ordinal, which it lessens by half, as: hálft fjórða hundrað (*half the fourth hundred*) 350; hálf önnur alin *an ell and a half;* hálfr annarr *one and a half;* hann var þar varla hálfan annan dag *he was there hardly a day and a half.*

Adjectives are formed from cardinal numerals with various significations, as: þrítugr, *consisting of thirty,* thus; þrítugsaldr 30 *years of age,* þrítugt skip *a ship with* 30 *pair of oars.* When added to numerals indicative of age *hálft,* as just explained, has a diminutive power, as: hálf þrítugr 25 *years old,* the reason of which is, that the Icelanders reckon by 10 (*tugr*), therefore hálf þrítugr is, 2½ *times* 10 = 25, and so on throughout. See p. 57.

CHAPTER II.

ON THE VERBS.

In the position of the verb and the employment of the different tenses considerable freedom prevails: thus the verb can be placed before the subject or after it, at discretion, as: ferr nú þjóðólfr til fundar við Brand; *now Thjódólfr goes to meet Brandr;* segir hann þá Huldarsögn, *then he relates the tradition of Hulda;* sváfu menn þá af of náttina, *the men slept during that night.* Likewise in narrative style the present and preterite are often interchanged, and arbitrarily so in the same sentence, as: en er Sturla fór til skips, var útkominn Hallvarðr Gullskór; *fann* hann þórð mág sinn á þingvelli, *segir* hann honum tíðindi, *but when Sturla went to his ship, Hallvarðr Gullskór had come out; he found Thordr his brother-in-law at Thingvalla; he tells him the tidings;* þórólfr ok Eyvindr *kómu* heim of haustit, *fór* Thórólfr til föður síns, *taka* þeir feðgar þá tal sín í milli, *spyrr* þórólfr eptir, &c. *Thórólfr and Eyvindr came home in the autumn; Thórólfr went to his father's; father and son then talk together; Thórólfr asks after,* &c.

An adverb which belongs to a verb is placed before the object and as near to the verb as possible, as: þá tók Randver hauk sinn ok plokkaði *af* fjaðrarnar, *then Randver took his hawk and plucked off its feathers;* hratt hon þá *fram* skipinu *then she launched forth the ship.* If the verb stand last, in a relative position, for instance, the adverb or preposition is put immediately before the verb, as: Jörmunrekr sá hauk þann, er hinn hafði fjaðrarnar *af* plokkat, *Jörmunrekr saw the hawk whose feathers had been plucked off;* hann var á skipi því er hon haíði *fram* hrundit, *he was on the ship which she had launched forth.*

The present participle in *-andi, -anda,* besides its usual active signification, contains also the idea of the future participle passive, and thus corresponds with the Latin present participle in *-ans, -ens, -ntis,* and the future participle passive in *-andum, -endum* both in meaning and form, as: allter segjanda sínum vin, *every thing may be said to one's friend;* varðveitandi eru boðorð Guðs, *God's commandments must be kept;* varla er trúanda *it is hardly credible;* knèfalla með upphaldandi höndum *to fall on one's knees with uplifted hands;* þetta er þiggjanda, *this is to be received;* á deyanda degi, *on the day of one's death.*

The future is formed by the auxiliary verbs *skal,* and still more frequently *mun* (will), and the infinitive of the principal verb: vit várum fœddir á einni nátt, ok mun skamt verða milli dauða okkars, *we were born in one night, and it will not be long between our deaths;* brœðr munu berjask *brothers will contend with each other.*

The perfect and pluperfect are formed by the auxiliary verb *hafa* and the perfect participle of the principal verb in the neuter: hann hafði veitt í einu höggi otr ok lax, *he had killed at one blow both otter and salmon;* Egill hafði gengit yfir skóg nökkurn, *Egill had gone over some wood.* If there be an object in the sentence the participle must take the gender and number of the object: þeir höfðu felldan höfðingja liðsins *they had struck down the chieftains of the people*. See p. 60. Some intransitive verbs use *vera* instead of *hafa*; er nökkur stund var liðin, *when some time had passed*, and then the participle of course takes the gender and number of the subject.

When *þú* immediately follows a verb the suffix *sk* in reflective verbs may coalesce with *þú* and become *stu*: snústu frá illu, *turn thyself from evil*; lægstu (*abase thyself*) at upp hefistu (*that thou mayest be exalted*); at eigi lægistu, þá er þú hyggr upp at hefjask, *that thou be not abased, when thou expectest to be honoured*; gerstu höfðingi fyrir liðinu, *make thyself leader of the host*; fástu vel at virði, *provide thyself well with victuals*.

Ek is often suffixed to the verb, and softens its *k* into *g*, as: *barðag* for *barða ek*, or if the verbal *root* has *gg*, these letters are changed into *kk*, as: *hykk* for *hygg ek*; sometimes *a* of the inflection is resolved into *i*, as: *ætlig* for *ætla ek*, *nemik* (*pres. conj.*) for *nema ek*.

The accusative with the infinitive is a frequent form of expression: væni engi maðr Ólaf konung því or landi farit hafa, *let no one fancy that King Ólafr therefore has gone out of the country*; satt hygg ek mik segja, *methinks I speak the truth*; ask veit ek standa, *I know that an ash-tree stands* (there); þik kvazk (*i. e.* kvað sik) hilmir hitta vilja, *the king said he wanted to meet with thee*.

Many verbs which imply the setting of something in motion require the object in the dative, as: kasta (steini, spjóti), verpa *to throw* (áðr þú verpir *söðli* af mar, *before thou throwest the saddle from the horse*), stinga, leggja *to stab* (hann lagði *spjóti* gegnum hann, *or*, hann lagði hann *spjóti he sent the spear through him*), skjóta *to shoot* (hann skaut manninn *öru*, hann skaut fyrir sik *skildi*), bregða (hann brá sverði *he drew his sword*), sá (sá korni *to sow corn*), blása, fnæsa *to blow out* (fnæsa eitri), spýta (hann spýtti upp miðinum í kerin *he spat up the mead into the vessels*, snúa, venda, skifta *to divide*. Most verbs likewise which signify rule, command, leniency, or the opposite govern the object in the dative, as: Gylfi konungr rèð löndum; hann bauð honum at láta skírask; at bjarga lífi; at eira konum ok kirkjum; at týna lífinu; koma as a transitive verb likewise governs in the dative, as: koma einum í vandræði *to bring one into peril;* ek kem því eigi við *I cannot apply it.*

Those verbs which signify a want, desire, or possession mostly govern the genitive with accusative of the person, and genitive of the thing, *e. g.*, sakna ek míns málvinar, *I miss my companion;* at spyrja einhvern ráðs *to ask one's advice;* at biðja hann friðar *to ask him for peace;* at afla fjár *to obtain property;* hann fèkk þeirrar konu er þórun hèt *he got to wife a woman called Thórun;* hann beið byrjar *he waited for a fair wind.*

The conjunctive is used when condition is implied, chiefly in dependent sentences after conjunctions, as: þó at or þótt *although,* ef *if;* likewise when a wish or desire is expressed: þó at hann væri eigi kominn, *though he may not have come;* en þó svá væri, *but though it be so;* vilda ek at þèr lærðit mik *I would that you taught me.* The present or preterite conjunctive may be used without a conjunction when it can be translated by *in case,* or *if; e. g.,* vili hann ekki með góðu, þá komdu til mín *will he not come by fair means, then do thou come to me;* kæmi hann meðan ek em á brottu, *should he come whilst I am away.*

CHAPTER III.

ON THE PARTICLES.

1. *Interrogative Particles.* The principal of these are: hví *why, wherefore,* hversu, hvè, hvernin, hvernig, meaning *how,* hvaða *what kind of,* as, hvaða maðr *what kind of man?* The older tongue mostly employs *hvat* instead, with the genitive plural, or the preposition *af,* as hvat manna, hvat af mönnum, hvar *where,* hvert *whither,* hvaðan *whence,* nær and hvenær *when,* hvárt or hvert *whether;* hvárt — eða or hvárt sem — eða *whether — or?*

2. *Negative Particles.* Simple negation is expressed by *nè* or *ne,* the prefixes *ó* or *ú,* and the suffixes *-gi, -at, -a.*

Nè or *ne* stands immediately before the word to which it belongs, and this must be a verb*, as: sól þat ne vissi,

* Einn is the only word not a verb before which *ne* is used; ne einn *none* (Old English *ne ane*) more frequently contracted into *neinn.*

hvar hon sali átti, *the sun knew not where she* had her dwelling;* máni þat ne vissi hvat hann megins átti *the moon knew not what might he had. Neither — nor* may be expressed by hvarki -nè, *or* nè -ne.

Ú or *ó,* answering to English *un, mis,* appears as a prefix before substantives, adjectives, participles and adverbs, as: ú-fúss *or* ó-fúss *unwilling,* ó-happ *or* ú-happ *misfortune.* See p. 89.

-gi and *-at* are always affixed to words; *-gi* to nouns and adverbs, *-at* to verbs, as: Loptki þat veit (Loptr eigi þat veit); Úlfgi hefir ok vel *Loptr knew it not, Úlfr has not also acted rightly;* verðrat iss á á *there is no ice on the river.*

When *-gi* is added to masculine nouns the noun-inflection *-r* is omitted, *e. g.,* Loptki, Úlfgi; and when *g* comes into immediate contact with a liquid, it is changed into *k,* as Loptki, hittki.

-a or *-at* occurs in the following cases:

1. the *first pers. sing.* always includes the pronoun which appears between the verb and the negation, as: fan-k-a *I found not, i. e.,* fann-ek-a (from finna *to find*); á-k-a *I have not* (from eiga *to own*); kveð-k-a *I say not* (from kvæða); naut-k-a *I enjoyed not* (from njóta); erumk-a *I am not.* The pronoun is often repeated, as: vil-k-at ek *I will not;* em-k-at ek *I am not:*
2. the *first pers. plur.* has no pronoun suffixed, and *-a* is added as a negative: erum-a *we are not;* ættim-a *we had not:*
3. in the *first pers. sing. subjunctive* the *k* of the pronoun is softened into *g,* as: myn-di-g-a *I would not:*
4. in the *second pers. sing.* (*ind.* or *subj.*) *-a* is suffixed and the pronoun omitted if the verb ends in *-r,* as: kallar-a *thou callest not* (from kalla *to call*); if it however terminates in *-t,* then *-at* stands with the pronoun after it, as: ert *thou art;* ert -at -tú *thou art not;* veitst -at -tú *thou knowest not:*
5. the imperative usually appends *-at* with the pronoun *þú,* as: kjósattú *choose not,* vaxattú *grow not.* When the con-

---

* In Norse, as well as German, the sun is of the feminine, and the moon of the masculine gender.

necting vowel *i* occurs in the verb it is retained in the negation, as: kvelj-at:

6. *-a* or *-at* is suffixed to the 3rd *pers. sing.*, as: er-a *he is not;* skal-a *he shall not*; verðr-at *he becomes not.*
7. When the 3rd *pers. plur.* ends in *-a*, only *t* is added, as: bita -t *they bite not;* to the ending *u*, however, of the 3rd *pers. plur.* either *-at* is appended, as: lètu-at (from láta *to let*), or -t, as: eigu-t, eru-t.
8. When *-i* terminates the 3rd *pers. sing. pret.* of verbs of the 2nd class, *-t* is suffixed, and usually *-a* in the subjunctive, as: varnaði *he hindered,* varnaðit *he hindered not;* bíti *should he bite,* bítia *should he not bite.*

The above cases concern only the ancient tongue; in the modern language eigi *or* ekki *not* is used.

The phrase "notwithstanding" or "nevertheless" is expressed by *eigi at heldr.*

Adverbs are formed from adjectives by the termination

-a, as: gjarna *willingly,* viða *widely,* illa *badly,* görva *quite,* heima *at home:*

-an, as: drjúgan *frequently,* jafnan *always,* gjarnan *willingly,* harðan *hardly:*

-liga, from adjectives ending in *-ligr*, as: knáligr *brave,* knáliga *bravely,* stórligr, stórliga *in a high degree.* This termination is often shortened into *-la,* as: harla (for harðla, harðliga) *very greatly,* varla *scarcely.*

Adverbs are also formed,

1. from the nom. and acc. neutr. of adjectives, as: trautt *with difficulty,* mest *mostly;*
2. from substantives by the termination
   -is, as: áleiðis *on the way,* andsœlis *opposite to the sun,* andstreymis *against the stream,* forvindis *before the wind,* jafnfœtis *of equal birth;*
   -veg, as: annanveg *otherwise,* from vegr *way,* þannveg *this wise,* hvernveg *how, in what way:* sometimes *v* is dropt, thus, þanneg, hverneg, or more usually, þannig, hvernig;
3. from the genitive case of substantives, as: loks *at last,* allskyns *all kinds of,* annarstaðar *elsewhere,* allskostar *in all respects,* útansóknar *out of a parish;*
4. from the dative case of substantives, as: öðruvísi *otherwise.*

Prepositions with the cases governed by them are used

adverbially, as: til hlitar *enough*, til sanns *truly*, með öllu *altogether*, á braut *away*.

Adverbs which signify motion from a place:
heiman *from home*, ofan *from above*, neðan *from below*, innan *from within*;
motion to a place:
hingat *hither*; þángat *thither*;
rest in a place:
uppi *above*, niðri *below*, inni *within*, úti *out*, frammi *before*, fjærri *far*; motion towards, partly presence on, the spot:
norðr *northwards*, suðr *southwards*, vestr *westwards*, austr *eastwards* as, hann gekk austr *he went eastwards*, hann var þá austr í landit *he was then in the east of the country*, niðr *downwards*, aptr *back again*.

The addition of *-na* to adverbs intensifies the idea expressed in the primitive, as: núna *this very moment*, hèrna *in this very place*, þanna *just there*, enna *just now*.

Some adverbs may be compared in the same way as adjectives, as:

soon	skamt	skemr	skemst	*widely*	viða	viðar	viðast
far	fjarri	firn	first	*frequently*	titt	tiðar	tiðast
often	opt	optar	optast	*seldom*	sjaldan	sjaldnar	sjaldnast.

Many irregular adjectives are, as adverbs, compared regularly, as:

northerly	norðr	norðar	norðast	*without*	út	útar	yzt
southerly	suðr	sunnar	syðst	*within*	in	innar	innst
easterly	austr	austar	austast	*up*	uppi	ofar	efst
westerly	vestr	vestar	vestast	*beneath*	niðri	neðar	neðst.

The following adverbs are irregular:

good	vel	betr	bezt,	*little*	litt	minnr	minst,
bad	illa	verr	verst,	*rather*	gjarna	heldr	helzt,
much	mjök	meirr	mest,	*within*	inni	innar	innst.

Lengi *long*, lengr *longer*, is used only of time; lengra, of place, lengst both of time and place.

Of the prepositions, some govern either the genitive, dative, or accusative; others govern both the dative and accusative.

The following govern in the genitive:

til *to*, án *without*, auk *besides*, and the compound or derived forms ámilli, ámeðal, ámillim, millum, millim *between*; sakir, fyrir sakir / sakar / sökum } *by means of, for the sake of*, vegna *on account of,* útan *without, beyond,* innan *within,* also *megin,* used with compounds as, báðu megin *on both sides* (*of anything*), í stað *instead of.*

The following take the dative:

af *of,* frá *from,* hjá *by, with* (French *chez,* Germ. *bei*), úr *out of,* undan *from, away from,* gagnvart *over against,* á mót, mót, í móti *against, towards,* ásamt *together with:*

with some combinations, as:

út af, upp frá, fram úr, á undan *before,* framhjá *by, over,* í gegn *against,* á hendr *against* (*in opposition*), til handa *for, for the best.*

The following govern in the accusative:

um (*of*) *about, concerning,* with all its compounds, whether it stands first or last, as: *umfram* or *fram um,* í gegnum *through,* fram yfir *over and above,* fram undir *until, up to,* and all those which are compounded from fyrir with an adverb of place in *-an,* as: fyrir norðan *to the north of,* fyrir útan bœinn *outside the town.* In ancient poetry *um* and *of* are occasionally found with the dative.

The following govern the dative and accusative according to their meaning:

á *on, upon,* í *in, to,* með *with,* við *with, by, at,* eptir *after,* fyrir *before,* undir *under,* yfir *over.*

Those which signify rest at a place mostly take the dative, as: konungr var á skipi *the king was on the ship,* þeir lágu í höfninni *they lay in the harbour,* and those which denote motion to a place employ the accusative as: hann gekk á skip *he went to the ship,* sigldu þeir um í höfnina *they sailed into the harbour;* but as they do not always refer to a place, the following definitions require attention.

Á takes the dative when used of a specified time, as: á hverju ári *every year,* á hverri nóttu *every night,* as well as in speaking of a certain day in the week *e.g.,* á laugardegi *on a Saturday:*

when it means *about, of, with, by,* in a figurative sense, as: fá þekking á einhverju *to obtain knowledge about everybody,* ek em á þeirri trú *I am of that faith,* hann lifir á málaferlum *he lives by lawsuits,* hún hefir aðra meðferð á kúm *she has another method with cows.*

Á takes the accusative when it signifies "on this wise, with respect to", as: á þann hátt, á þá leið *in that manner,* á aðra síðuna *on the other side*, at mæla á danska tungu *to speak in the Danish language*, hann lá á bakit *he lay on his back*; but if á bakinu were said, it would mean *upon the back* (*of some one else*). Likewise in the signification of "in upon, in towards, above", as: renna á *to run in upon*, at snara á norrænn *to translate into Norse*.

Á may be used in the dative or accusative with regard to periods of time, as: á haustum, sumrum, *or* á haustin, sumrin *in autumn, summer*.

Í takes the dative when it means *at*, *in*, as: konungr var þá ekki í bœnum *the king was not then at prayers*.

Í mostly governs the accusative in determining time, as: í þann tíma *at that time*, í annat sinn *at another time*. Moreover, í þeirri svipan, í því bili *at that moment*, can be said.

Með takes the dative in the sense of a means or instrument, as: fjötraðr með hlekkjum myrkranna *fettered with chains of darkness*;

when it means *with*, *among*, as: gott þykkir mèr með þèr at vera *methinks it is good to be with thee*; landit var skipt með þeim *the land was shared amongst them*;

when it signifies *along*, as: suðr með landi *southwards along the country*; *along with*, as: hann gekk út með konu sinni *he went out along with his wife*;

by means of, as: hann sýndi með hugprýði sinni at, &c., *he showed through his courage that*, &c.

Með governs the accusative when the object is regarded as lifeless, or involuntarily accompanying, as: hann kom með bókina *he came with the book*, þá fóru menn ámóti hánum með mann fjötraðan *then men went towards him with a fettered man*.

Við requires the dative in the signification of *against*, as: at taka við einum *to take against one*.

It takes the accusative when used of *place*, or answers to *at*, *by*, *with*, as: við garðin *at the farm*, ek talaði lengi við hann *I talked a long time with him*.

Sometimes *með* and *við* are interchanged, and their government is guided by their signification.

Eptir takes the dative when it means *according to*, *along with*, as: eptir þeirri reglu *according to this rule*, þeir riðu eptir ánni *they rode along the river*.

It governs the accusative when it expresses relation of time or order, as: eptir miðjan dag *after midday*, þeir tóku allan arf eptir fõdur sinn *they succeeded to their father's inheritance*.

Fyrir governs the dative when it means *before*, *in the presence of*, *on account of*, or when it betokens hindrance, as: hann talaði langt erendi fyrir liðinu *he delivered a lengthy message to the people*, ek gat ekki verið í friði fyrir hánum *I could not be at peace for him*, látast fyrir einum *to perish by one's own hand*, hann þorði ekki fyrir hundinum *he dared not for the dogs*.

It takes the accusative when used of time, as: litlu fyrir vetr *shortly before winter*; when it means *instead of*, *for*, as: hann sendi mann fyrir sik *he sent some one in his stead*;

when it signifies *by means of*, *by*, as: verða sáluhólpinn fyrir trúna *to be saved by faith*; when used of price, as: hvað gafstu fyrir bœkrnar *what didst thou give for the books?*

Undir takes the dative after it in the signification of *rest in a place*, as: undir borðinu, stólnum *under the table*, *the chairs*;

when it means *under*, *subordinate to*, *dependent upon*, as: alla þá sem undir hánum eru *all that are under him*, þat er ekki undir því komit *that is not of great consequence*.

It has the accusative in the signification of *away towards*, as: undir sólarlag *towards sunset*, and *away under*, as: undir eyna *away under the island*.

Yfir governs the dative when it betokens *rest in a place*, as: yfir eldinum *above the fire*;

when it means to have power over, as: drottna yfir landi *to rule over a country*.

It takes the accusative when it means *motion to a place*, as: hann rœr út yfir nesit *he rows around the naze*;

in the signification of *more than*, as: mèr unni mær yfir mann hvern *the girl loved me more than any one else*.

At *or* að is the only preposition which governs the three cases.

It governs the genitive when used in the meaning of *at the place of*, *with any one*, *at his house* (the word *húsi* or the like being understood), as: þeir gistu at Bjarnar *they were Björn's guests*. Formerly this preposition was used with the genitive of the personal pronouns, as: þeir gistu at mín, þín *with me, thee.*

It takes the dative when it means *to a place,* as: koma at bœ *to come to a farm:*

at a place, as: at lögbergi *at the council-hill;* hann bjó at Birgisheimi *he lived at Birgisheimr:*

transition from one state to another, as: hann varð at steini *he was changed into stone;* brenna at ösku *to burn to ashes:*

before comparatives, as: váru þeir at vaskari *were they the braver.*

a future time, as: liðr at jólum *Jule approaches,* at hausti *next autumn.*

This preposition, when it governs the dative case, likewise forms many adverbial expressions.

It employs the accusative when it means *behind, after* (*one's death*), as: láta eitt at sik *to leave something behind one;* at föður sinn *after his father* (*his death*). Thus in Runic inscriptions, reisa stein at einn *to raise a stone to one.*

Many names of places occur in the dative with the preposition *á, í* or *at,* instead of the nominative after *heita* or the like, as: sá bær hèt á Steini *that house was called Stone;* hann bjó í kaupstað þeim er heitir í Stafangri *he lived in the market-town which is called Stavanger.*

CHAPTER IV.

OF ELLIPSES.

Ellipses or omissions frequently occur in Old-Norse. In most cases they are easily supplied, as for instance, when the pronouns *sá, sú, hann, hún* or *þat* are omitted, the subject or object for which they are used having been already named: siðan sneið Karkr höfuð af jarli ok hljóp í braut með (þat), *afterwards Karkr cut off the jarl's head, and ran off with* (*it*).

The 3rd *pers.* of the verb is often used without a subject, when this is unknown, or can be easily supplied, as. svá segir í Grimnismál, *it is thus said in Grimnismál.*

The word kostr *choice, alternative, resource* is often elided in sentences the meaning of which is clear, as: far eptir, Háleyíngr, sá mun þèr hinn bezti (kostr) vera, *pursue, Háleyingr, thy best alternative;* ok er sá (kostr) til, at sigla undan, *and the only choice is to sail away.*

The verbs *vera* and *verða* are frequently dropt, as well as the definite forms, as: einn morginn vakti Ástríðr Glúm ok sagði at nauta fjöldi Sigmundar var kominn í tún ok vildi brjóta andvirki: "en ek hefi eigi fráleik til at reka (hann) í braut, en verkmenn (eru) at vinnu", *one morning Ástríðr awoke Glúmr, and said, that a lot of Sigmundr's cattle had got into the meadow, and would throw down the cocks; "but I am not nimble enough to drive (them) away, and the workmen are at work"*.

These ellipses take place especially after the words *mun* and *skal* in the future, as: þá mun hann kominn (vera) til konungs, *then will he have come to the king*; þarí skulu ok talin nöfn þeirra, *therein shall their names also (be) reckoned.*

Sometimes the ellipsis is more important, *e. g.*, Glúmr segir, sá ek glöggt hvat títt var: (þú ert) barn at aldri, en (hefir þó) vegit slíka hetju sem þorvaldr var, *I saw clearly how the matter stood: (thou art) a child in age, but (yet hast) slain such a hero as Thorvaldr was.*

PART IV.
PROSODY.

CHAPTER I.

Old-Norse poetry is not regulated like that of ancient Greece and Rome by quantity, but by accentuation, which cannot, however, be arbitrarily laid upon any syllable. In a word consisting of many syllables, the accent must rest on that which usually has the tone: in monosyllables it cannot fall on prepositions and conjunctions, except when it becomes emphatic.

Icelandic poems are divided into regular strophes (erendi, vísa*, staka) which generally contain eight lines (orð, vísuorð). These strophes are subdivided into halves (vísuhelmingr), and each of these again into two parts (vísufjórðungr) constituting a quarter strophe or couplet.

* Vísa, like the German *Weise*, means the manner or *wise* of doing a thing: this wise, otherwise.

CHAPTER II.

ALLITERATION.

Alliteration, or letter-rhyme, is an essential characteristic of Old-Norse poetry. Consonantal alliteration requires three words or accented syllables in a couplet to have the same initial letter (ljóðstafr), and two of these words to occur in in the former hemistich, and the other in the latter. The initial letter of the last which generally commences the line, and must always stand as near the beginning of it as possible, is called *höfuðstafr* (headstaff) or *chief* letter, being that which governs the others: the sub-letters have no fixed position. The initials of the words placed in the first line are called *stuðlar* (props or stays) because they support or give force to the cardinal letter, of which they may be regarded as the auxiliaries, thus:

*f*yllisk *f*jörvi	*filled with the life-blood*
*f*eigra manna.	*of doomed men.*

Here the three *f*s are *ljóðstafir* or rhyme-letters; the chief letter (höfuðstafr) is in *f*eigra, and the sub-letters (stuðlar) occur in *f*yllisk and *f*jörvi.

One or more particles, or short words, may be introduced into the beginning of the second hemistich, only they must be unaccented, thus:

er á *G*autlandi *g*engum	*when to Gothland we went*
at *G*rafvitnis morði;	*to give death to the serpent;*

here *at* is the augmentative participle.

When the *höfuðstafr* begins with a double or compound consonant as *sk*, *sp*, *st*, the *stuðlar* must consist, if possible, of the same letters; this rule applies especially to the above compounds, as:

beit í *Sk*arpa *sk*erjum	*struck on Skarpa's cliff*
*sk*eribildr at hjaldri;	*the sword in battle;*

or:

*sk*orin var *Sk*öglar kápa	*scored was the coat of mail*
at *sk*jöldunga hjaldri	*in the battle of the kings.*

Here *sk* are the rhyme-letters, and *gr* in the following distich:

þá var *gr*und *gr*óin	*then was the ground green*
*gr*ænum lauki;	*with green herb.*

In short lines one of the sub-letters is often omitted, but the chief-letter never:

*h*ljóðs bið' k'allar
*h*elgar kindir;

to attention I bid all
holy generations:

*g*ól um Ásum
*G*ullinkambi

crowed near the Æsir
Gullinkambi (the golden-combed).

Vowels interchange with each other, and should, if possible, be different:

*ö*nd þau nè *á*ttu;
*ó*ð þau nè höfðu;

breath they possessed not;
sense they had not.

Here *ö*, *á*, and *ó* form a complete and elegant letter-rhyme.

J, *v*, and *k*, when followed by a vowel, are admitted into the number of correspondent letters:

*e*k man *j*ötna
*á*r umborna;

I remember the giants
born in the beginning.

Here *e*, *j*, *á* rhyme with each other: examples in which *v* answers to vowels are extremely rare:

svaf *v*ætr Freyja
*á*tta nóttum;

slept not Freyja
for eight nights.

Here *v* and *á* correspond.

Sometimes we meet with verses in which such words as *úlfr, rangr, reiðr,* which in the earliest times began with *v*, have formed alliteration with words beginning with this letter, as in Atlaqviða:

*v*ín í *V*alhöll
(*v*) reiði sásk þeir Húna;

wine in Valhalla.
They feared the Huns' wrath;

and in Baldrsdrauma:

(*V*) rindr berr
í *V*estrsölum;

Rindr (Vala's mother) bears
in the western halls.

When there is an unequal line, or a solitary member in a verse, such as the third and sixth lines of the six-membered stanzas, it always contains two alliterated words, as in the following quotation from Vafþrúdnismál:

or Ýmis holdi
var jörð umsköpuð,
  en or *b*einum *b*jörg,
himinn or hausi
ins hrímkalda jötuns,
  en or *s*veita *s*jór.

of Ymir's flesh
the earth was shaped,
  of his bones the mountains;
heaven of the skull
of the hoar-frosty giant;
  and of his sweat the sea.

CHAPTER III.

ASSONANCES.

Assonance, or line-rhyme, is called in Old-Norse poetry *hending*, and is divided into two kinds, whole and half-assonance.

Whole-assonance, or properly speaking, consonance (*aðalhending* noble rhyme), occurs when two syllables in the same line have the vowels and the consonants immediately following them alike, as: s*um*-ir (some) and g*um*-ar (men), m*erk*-i (mark) and st*erk*-a (strong).

Half-assonance (*skothending* imperfect rhyme) admits of different vowels followed by the same consonants, as, st*irð*um (*dat. plur.* of stirðr *stiff*) and n*orð*an, v*arð* (I became) and f*orð*a (to guard). The half-assonance is commonly used in the first line of the couplet which contains the sub-letters, and the whole-assonance in the latter hemistich, as:

fast*orð*r skyli f*irð*a	*word-fast should the king be*
f*eng*sæll vera þ*eng*ill;	*who will keep warriors;*
hæfir heit at r*júf*a	*to break thy plighted faith*
hj*ald*ur mögnuðr! þèr *ald*ri.	*beseems thee not, mighty man!*

All syllables which have an assonance, must be accented; all consonants may form part of an assonance except the flexional endings *r* and *s* after consonants: accordingly bj*arts* and hj*arta* are a regular whole-assonance, and *dð*r and fl*ýð*i a correct half-assonance.

Rhyme is important in determining the right orthography and pronunciation of a word. For instance, as there is a whole-assonance in the line t*ír*arlaust ok *Í*ra, it is clear that *tír* must rhyme with *ír*, and cannot be written with *ý*, which has been incorrectly used by some writers.

CHAPTER IV.

RHYME.

The terminating rhyme of the Icelanders is formed on the same principle as that of the poetry of other nations. Final rhymes are single or compound, being either formed by the ultimate, as: *far, var, í, því,* or by both the ultimate and penultimate together, as: *auka, lauka, segja, þegja.* There is no instance before the Reformation, in which the first line is rhymed with the third, and the second with the fourth, only consecutive rhyming lines being met with previously to that period.

Such words as *sparat* and *kverit, varð* and *orð* are admissible as half-rhymes, because they have the same final consonants, though their vowels are unlike.

CHAPTER V.

OF THE DIFFERENT KINDS OF VERSE.

The ancient Icelanders divided their poems into three chief classes, called *Fornyrðalag, Dróttkvæði,* and *Rúnhenda.* The first possesses only alliteration, the second, alliteration and assonance, the third, alliteration and final rhyme.

1. Fornyrðalag, or, Narrative Verse.

The original and simplest form of versification in Old-Norse, which it also possesses in common with the other Teutonic languages, particularly the Anglo-Saxon, is *Fornyrðalag* (old word-lay) which is the most unrestricted in its metre, having the greatest *complement**, and frequently only one auxiliary letter. All the poems of the Elder Edda are in narrative verse. It is divided into two kinds, the *Starkaðarlag proper,* and *Ljóðaháttr.*

The *Starkaðarlag proper* consists of strophes of eight lines connected by alliteration: each line has two long syllables, or two resting-points for the voice; the rhyme-letters should be three, though one of the sub-letters is often wanting. The following stanza from the Vǫluspá offers an example of narrative verse thus constructed:

ek sá Baldri	*I foresaw for Balder,*
blóðgum tívor,	*for that bloody victim,*
Óðins barni	*for that son of Odin*

---

* Short precursory words which, though independent of the structure of the verse, are necessary to the completion of the sense, constitute what may be called the *complement* (*málfylling* verse-filling).

orlög fólgin;	*the fate hid for him.*
stóð umvaxinn	*There stood growing*
völlum hæri	*above the valley*
mjór ok mjök fagr	*a slender and very fair*
mistilsteinn.	*mistletoe.*

The want of one of the sub-letters in the 1, 3, and 5 line constitutes a deviation from the strict rule; there is no complement in the above instance. On the other hand, the following strophe is very irregular:

Hvat er með Ásum?	*What are the Æsir (gods) doing?*
Hvat er með Álfum?	*What are the Elves doing?*
Gnýr allr Jötunheimr;	*Bellows all Jötunheimr;*
Æsirru á þingi.	*the Æsir are in council.*
Stynja dvergar	*Groan the dwarfs*
fyr steindurum	*at the cavern door,*
veggbergs vísir.	*the sages of the mountain.*
Vituð èr enn eða hvat?	*Know you it? But what?*

which should be thus intoned in reading:

Hvat'r með Ásum?
Hvat'r með Álfum?
Gnýr allr Jöt'nheimr;
Æs'rr' á þingi.

Stynja dvergar
fyr) steindurum
veggbergs vísir.
Vit'ð èr enn eð' hvat?

There are complements in verses 3 and 6. The contraction of so many syllables into one in the 4th line is peculiar, and the last line has 3 toned syllables, which is contrary to all rule, and might be regarded as a corruption, did not the same discrepancy occur in less than seven times in the Völuspá, and always at the end of the strophe.

As a variation from the *Starkaðarlag proper* there is the *hnept* or *stýft* (shortened) *Fornyrðalag;* which has the first of the two lines either trisyllabic, and all the three syllables commonly long, or ends with an intoned monosyllable.

The following stanza from Egils Sonartorrek furnishes an example:

era auðþeyst;	*it cannot easily happen;*
þvíat) ekki veldr	*because the difficult*
höfugligr	*silent desire*
or) hyggju stað	*of the three sons*
þagnafundr	*once born*

þriggja niðja	*in Jötunheimr*
árborinn	*cannot easily*
or) Jötunheimum.	*be drawn from the breast.*

Another kind of *Fornyrðalag* in frequent use is *Ljóðaháttr,* consisting of a six-lined strophe, whose 1st, 2nd, 4th, and 5th lines are constructed like the *Starkaðarlag proper,* having two resting-points, pauses, or long syllables, and connected by alliteration; but the 3rd and 6th line have three pauses with a special alliteration: each of these lines has 2 (very rarely 3) rhyme-letters different from those of the two preceding lines, as:

ölr ek varð	*drunk I became,*
varð) ofrölvi	*became very drunken*
at ins fróða Fjalars;	*in the giant's dwelling;*
því er) öldr baztr,	*for best is ale*
at) aptr ofheimtir	*when again recovers*
hverr sitt geð gumi.	*each man his wit.*

The following stanza offers an example of a metre with three rhyme-letters:

ungr var'k forðum;	*young was I once;*
fór'k einn saman,	*went I quite alone,*
þá) varð ek villr vega;	*then went I astray;*
auðigr þóttumsk	*I thought myself happy*
er'k annan fann;	*when I found another:*
maðr er manns gaman:	*man is the sport of man.*

The following half-strophe is peculiarly composed:

þat'r þá *r*eynt,	*that is then proved*
er þú at) *r*únum spyrr	*when thou askest of runes*
inum) *r*eginkunnum:	*to the gods alone known.*

Here the three rhyme-letters *r* are so placed that each line contains one.

When the eight-lined *Fornyrðalag* is so constructed that two half-rhymes occur in the first line of each couplet, and two whole-rhymes in the second line, it is called *Toglag*; for instance in the following half-strophe:

ok *senn sona*	*and then Canute slew,*
sl*ó* hvern ok þ*ó*	*or banished at once*
*Að*albr*áð*s e*ð*a	*each of the sons*
út flæmdi Kn*út*r:	*of Aðalbraðr.*

2. Dróttkvæði.

The metre usual in laudatory poems is called *Dróttkvæði* (from drótt *chief,* kvæði song) or "heroic verse", and was most commonly used by the skalds who lived after the 9th century. It has alliteration and assonance, and very rarely admits the *málfylling*. The chief letter must be the first in every second line, and the second rhyme in every line must occur in the penultimate syllable. The first strophe of the poem called *Geisli* the ray, an eulogium on King Olafr the Saint by Einarr Skularson, will furnish an example of this kind of metre:

eins má orð ok b*œn*ir
*all*sráðanda hins snj*all*a
vel er) fr*óð*r sá er getr g*óð*a
guðs þr*enn*ing mèr k*enn*a.
göfugt lj*ós* boðar g*eis*li
g*unn*ðfligr misk*unn*ar
ág*æt*an býð ek *ít*rum
*Ól*afi brag s*ól*ar.

The following is the order of the words: eins má mèr kenna orð ok bœnir, sá er vel fróðr, er getr góða þrenning hins snjalla allsráðanda guðs. Ek býð ítrum Ólafi ágætan brag. Gunnðfligr geisli boðar göfugt ljós miskunnar sólar; meaning, "Likewise can I know words as well as prayers; he is very wise who comprehends the glorious Trinity of Almighty God. I offer to noble Olafr an excellent song. A most powerful beam betokens the beautiful light of the sun of mildness (Christ)".

Assonances here occur in every line; in the first line of each couplet there is a half-rhyme, in the second, a whole one. There are three resting-points in each line, and a complement only in the 3rd line, *i. e. vel er*.

When a strophe, formed in other respects like the *Dróttkvæði*, has eight long syllables in each line, it is called *Hrynhenda,* as:

lj*ót*u varp á lypting *út*an
l*auð*ri; bifðísk gullit r*auð*a;
f*ast*ligr hneigði furu gl*æst*ri
f*yr*is garmr of skeiðar st*yr*i;
st*ír*ðum hèlt um Stafangr n*orð*an
st*ál*um; bifðusk fyrir *ál*ar;
*upp*i glóðu elmars t*ypp*i
*eld*i glík í Dana v*eld*i.

The order of the words is as follows: ljótu lauðri varp á útan lypting; gullit rauða bifðisk; fastligr fyris garmr of styri skeiðar hneigði furu glæstri; Stafangr hèlt um stirðum stálum norðan; álar bifðusk fyrir; uppi glóðu elmars typpi glík eldi í veldi Dana; meaning, "with boisterous sea-foam drifted on the prow of the vessel; the red gilded mast is shaken; the strong wind around the rudder bent sideways the ship splendidly adorned; Stafangr steered the rude prow northwards; the breakers are broken before (the proceeding ship); aloft shone the ship-masts like fire in the kingdom of the Danes".

---

3. Rúnhenda.

Rúnhenda (rún *poem*, henda *rhyme*) or "popular verse", has final rhyme along with alliteration. Each strophe consists of eight lines, the first determining the metre of the rest. This class of versification is subdivided into several kinds, according to the number of accentuated syllables. The following offers an example with two resting-points:

slíkt er svá:
siklingr á
öld þess ánn
orðróm þánn;
jarla er
austan ver
skatna skýrstr
Skúli dýrstr:

meaning, "Thus it is: the king possesses this fame; the people call it good; of the princes is Skúli (come) from the east, the worthiest man, of heroes the most excellent".

Another instance furnishes four accentuated syllables:

þiggja kná með gulli glöð
gotna ferð af ræsi mjöð,
drekka lætr hann sveit at sín
silfri skenkt it fagra vín;
greipum mætir gullin skál,
gumnum sendir Rínar bál,
eigi hitta æðra mann,
jarla beztr en skjöldung þann:

meaning, "The cheerful troop of men can receive with gold the mead from the king: he let the crowd drink in his (house) the goodly wine presented in silver; the golden goblet meets the hands (the hands seize it); to the men sends the best of princes the fire of the Rhine (gold); one meets not with a better man than this prince".

---

4. Refrain or Burden.

One or more verses which are repeated in a certain division of the poem constitute the refrain or burden (stef, viðkvæði), which varies greatly in its application; but mostly consists of two or more lines, separate from the strophe. Sometimes it occurs at the end of every strophe, and forms a species of chorus.

Printed by Breitkopf and Haertel, Leipzig.

Lightning Source UK Ltd.
Milton Keynes UK
29 November 2010

163613UK00010B/11/P